A WOMAN'S ALMANAC

YOUR GUIDE TO FEMINISM, ACTIVISM AND CHANGE

2019

ST. JOHN'S STATUS OF WOMEN COUNCIL

BREAKWATER
P.O. Box 2188, St. John's, NL, Canada, A1C 6E6
WWW.BREAKWATERBOOKS.COM

ISBN 978-1-55081-758-4
A CIP catalogue record for this book is available from Library and Archives Canada.

We acknowledge the support of the Canada Council for the Arts, which last year invested $153 million to bring the arts to Canadians throughout the country. We acknowledge the financial support of the Government of Canada and the Government of Newfoundland and Labrador through the Department of Business, Tourism, Culture and Rural Development for our publishing activities.

Printed and bound in Canada.

Canada Council for the Arts Conseil des Arts du Canada Canada Newfoundland Labrador

Cover and interior art on pages 1 and 36 by Robyn Flannigan

Robyn Flannigan is a graphic designer and illustrator with over five years of experience working with advertising agencies, small businesses, and nonprofit organizations. Currently based out of her home studio in St. John's, Newfoundland, she works with a variety of clients on everything from editorial illustration to branding. When she's not sketching, you can find Robyn exploring nature or catching up on the latest horror movies.

Breakwater Books is committed to choosing papers and materials for our books that help to protect our environment. To this end, this book is printed on a recycled paper that is certified by the Forest Stewardship Council®.

FSC www.fsc.org MIX Paper from responsible sources FSC® C016245

Thank you for purchasing *A Woman's Almanac*!

We just know you will  it!

Your support helps the St. John's Status of Women Council continue its feminist work in advancing gender justice and equality. We take great pride in carrying on the rich tradition of the women's movement in Newfoundland and Labrador.

You can learn more about our work at sjwomenscentre.ca

Jenny Wright (M.S.W., R.S.W.) is a feminist, activist, speaker and the Executive Director of the St. John's Status of Women Council as well as the current Co-Chair of the Provincial Action Network on the Status of Women in Newfoundland and Labrador. She has worked across Canada and New Zealand for more than 20 years in social justice – with a specific focus on gender equality and justice. She is a strong advocate against all forms of violence against women, including sex working, trans and Indigenous women. Jenny speaks frequently on how the underfunding of women's anti-violence organizations is a pervasive form of violence against women and has been called as a witness to the Federal Standing Committee on Violence Against Women. For the past four years she has co-led the organizing committee for the In Her Name Vigil for missing and murdered women of NL, and is a member of the Domestic Violence at Work Committee that is working towards the implementation of domestic violence leave legislation across Canada. Passionate about honouring women's history Jenny is a contributing editor of *A Woman's Almanac: Your Guide to Feminism, Activism and Change.*

"FEMINISM IS NOT SOMETHING WE WEAR.
IT'S SOMETHING **WE DO** AND WE DO IT EVERY DAY."

This year we were profoundly inspired by the women-led #MeToo, #TimesUp, and other grassroots movements that changed the way we move through the world.

We felt ourselves being lifted by strong women who, one after the other, stood and spoke their truth. We celebrated, we cried, we got angry, and we were inspired by the women who found the courage to say – "it stops here."

We dedicate this year's Almanac to those women who used their voice even when the cost was high, who overcame and encouraged us to speak out, or who spoke for us when we simply couldn't.

We hope the Almanac reminds you that you are not alone, that you are powerful in so many ways, and that your activism matters.

As always, this Woman's Almanac is dedicated to its original creator Marian Frances White, who steadfastly believed that the voices of Newfoundland and Labrador women were to be honoured and recorded.

Jenny Wright
Executive Director, St. John's Status of Women Council

Mary Shortall was elected president of the Newfoundland and Labrador Federation of Labour (NLFL) in October 2013. She is the former Atlantic regional director for the Canadian Labour Congress (CLC) and had been the Newfoundland representative for the CLC since 2001. She has been an activist, leader, facilitator, and curriculum developer throughout her forty-year involvement in the labour movement and sees education and political action as the key components of activism and change. Currently, Mary is board chair of the St. John's Status of Women Council (SJSWC), sits on the board of the Collaborative Applied Research in Economics (C.A.R.E.) at Memorial University, and the Masters of Employment Relations (M.E.R.) advisory committee. Mary defines herself as a feminist, a political activist, and a human-rights and workers'-rights advocate who is proud to work with so many others of like mind to "be the change she wants to see in the world." Mary enjoys hiking, yoga, fitness activities in general, travelling, reading, and riding her motorcycle.

WELCOME

Being part of an organization whose focus is creating equality for all women in a very unequal world has been an amazing experience for me. I am so proud and humbled by the passion and dogged determination of those in this struggle who keep on working towards that equality through the services they provide, along with their constant advocacy for real change. That work is constant, and tough, yet it is so necessary if we are ever to realize our dream.

One thing I have learned through my work is that our society will never achieve equality if we do not address and eliminate gender-based violence.

The joy in this struggle, and our hope for real change, happens when women and women identified everywhere begin to speak up and tell their stories.

Some of these stories are within the covers of this year's almanac, and I want to thank those courageous contributors for sharing their experiences.

I believe that the #metoo, #timesup, and #donewaiting movements have put pressure on decision makers the whole world over to recognize that the time for change is now.

Author Rebecca Solnit said, "Being unable to tell your story is living death. The right to speak is a form of wealth that is being redistributed. No wonder powerful men are furious."

Thank you for finding your voices, telling your stories, and turning our anger at such injustices into hope and action.

Because of you, and the continued work of those organizations dedicated to women's equality and their like-minded partners, we can dare to believe that another world is indeed possible. Thank you.

In sisterhood and solidarity,

Mary Shortall
Chair, SJSWC

JANUARY

FOCUS ON ONE OF YOUR STRENGTHS

CIRCLE ONE

I'm woke!

Having feelings

I'm awesome!

Idea crush

Fuck the patriarchy!

Did I self-care?

MONDAY	TUESDAY	WEDNESDAY
	1	2
7	8	9
14	15	16
21	22	23
28	29	30

WHAT HAVE YOU DONE FOR SELF-CARE THIS MONTH?

#FEMINISTFRIDAY
PAY IT FORWARD

HOW DID YOU RESIST?

THURSDAY	FRIDAY	SATURDAY	SUNDAY
3	4	5	6
10	11	12	13
17	18	19	20
24	25	26	27
31			

NOTES

JANUARY

M	T	W	T	F	S	S
	1	2	3	4	5	6
7	8	9	10	11	12	13
14	15	16	17	18	19	20
21	22	23	24	25	26	27
28	29	30	31	1	2	3

31 MONDAY

1 TUESDAY

New Year's Day

2 WEDNESDAY

THINGS TO DO

WEEKLY GOALS AND NOTES

3 THURSDAY

4 FRIDAY

5 SATURDAY

6 SUNDAY

Epiphany (Old Christmas Day)

THOUGHTS AND INSPIRATION

JANUARY

M	T	W	T	F	S	S
	1	2	3	4	5	6
7	8	9	10	11	12	13
14	15	16	17	18	19	20
21	22	23	24	25	26	27
28	29	30	31	1	2	3

7 MONDAY

8 TUESDAY

9 WEDNESDAY

THINGS TO DO

WEEKLY GOALS AND NOTES

10 THURSDAY

11 FRIDAY

12 SATURDAY

13 SUNDAY

THOUGHTS AND INSPIRATION

JANUARY

M	T	W	T	F	S	S
	1	2	3	4	5	6
7	8	9	10	11	12	13
14	15	16	17	18	19	20
21	22	23	24	25	26	27
28	29	30	31	1	2	3

14 MONDAY

15 TUESDAY

16 WEDNESDAY

THINGS TO DO

WEEKLY GOALS AND NOTES

17 THURSDAY

18 FRIDAY

19 SATURDAY

20 SUNDAY

THOUGHTS AND INSPIRATION

JANUARY

M	T	W	T	F	S	S
	1	2	3	4	5	6
7	8	9	10	11	12	13
14	15	16	17	18	19	20
21	22	23	24	25	26	27
28	29	30	31	1	2	3

21 MONDAY

22 TUESDAY

Trans Prisoner Day of Action

23 WEDNESDAY

THINGS TO DO

WEEKLY GOALS AND NOTES

24 THURSDAY

25 FRIDAY

26 SATURDAY

27 SUNDAY

THOUGHTS AND INSPIRATION

JANUARY

M	T	W	T	F	S	S
	1	2	3	4	5	6
7	8	9	10	11	12	13
14	15	16	17	18	19	20
21	22	23	24	25	26	27
28	29	30	31	1	2	3

28 MONDAY

STAMP OUT STIGMA

Mental Health Awareness Day

29 TUESDAY

30 WEDNESDAY

THINGS TO DO

WEEKLY GOALS AND NOTES

31 THURSDAY

women are strong as hell

THIS IS NOT YOUR TYPICAL SELF-CARE GUIDE
(#BORING SELF-CARE)

How many times have you read that you need to take a self-care day—that you should go to the gym, take a spa day, get a massage? A hundred, right? Well that would be fucking lovely if you had disposable income, Internet access, had time off between three jobs, could afford childcare, or weren't incarcerated. Sometimes the mainstream ideas around self-care can be more harmful than helpful. Sure, if you have the money to do spa days and take vacations, fill your boots. But let's talk about self-care in a way that can be more inclusive.

We need to talk about self-care when you have limited resources, when your options are few, when your mental health gets in the way, when you're living with a disability, or chronic pain and illness, or when you're in recovery. Oftentimes the traditional ways of self-care set people up for failure, because it becomes another thing on your growing to-do list that never gets done. Self-care is meant to be just that: caring for yourself, not another task or obligation. We would like to share some ideas of self-care that might be more inclusive and accessible for folks. Some of these ideas were shared with us from incarcerated women, who know best of all how to take care of yourself and others when resources are limited.

DO SOMETHING YOU ENJOY
(WRITE A POEM, PAINT, TAKE A WALK, SING A SONG, PHONE A FRIEND)

MAKE A MENTAL LIST OF THINGS YOU FEEL GRATEFUL FOR
(EVEN IF YOU'RE FEELING CROOKED)

PRACTICE POSITIVE SELF-TALK

CARVE OUT TIME FOR BASIC NEEDS
(DRINK WATER, EAT A MEAL, TAKE A BREATH)

WRITE A LETTER TO YOURSELF OR SOMEONE ELSE
(YOU DON'T HAVE TO SEND IT)

SPEND TIME WITH PEOPLE WHO YOU ENJOY BEING AROUND
(IF YOU LIKE PEOPLE)

- PRACTICE SELF-PLEASURE (YES, MASTURBATION)
- TAKE A MENTAL VACATION FROM WHATEVER YOU'RE DOING (EVEN FOR JUST FIVE MINUTES)
- SIT BY THE OCEAN (IF IT'S FIT TO BE OUTSIDE)
- DO SOME GENTLE STRETCHING (IF YOU'RE ABLE TO)
- TAKE A NAP (IF YOU DON'T HAVE TODDLERS)
- BREATHE IN THE FRESH AIR (OR FOG)
- TAKE A SHOWER (IF YOU WANT TO)
- MAKE YOUR BED (IF YOU HAVE THE LUXURY OF YOUR OWN SLEEPING SPACE)

Maybe none of these options work for you, and that's okay. Be kind to yourself even if you feel like you haven't been making self-care a priority. Not being hard on yourself is self-care, too.

Bridget Clarke is the Community Support Worker with Safe Harbour Outreach Project (SHOP), and has been working with the St. John's Status of Women Council for five years. Bridget studied Sociology with honours at Acadia University, and completed a Masters in Gender Studies at Memorial University of Newfoundland. Bridget loves dogs, gin, and supporting her local girl gang.

FEBRUARY

FOCUS ON ONE OF YOUR STRENGTHS

CIRCLE ONE

I'm woke!

Having feelings

I'm awesome!

Idea crush

Fuck the patriarchy!

Did I self-care?

MONDAY	TUESDAY	WEDNESDAY
4	5	6
11	12	13
18	19	20
25	26	27

WHAT HAVE YOU DONE FOR SELF-CARE THIS MONTH?

#FEMINISTFRIDAY
PAY IT FORWARD

HOW DID YOU RESIST?

THURSDAY	FRIDAY	SATURDAY	SUNDAY
	1	2	3
7	8	9	10
14	15	16	17
21	22	23	24
28			

NOTES

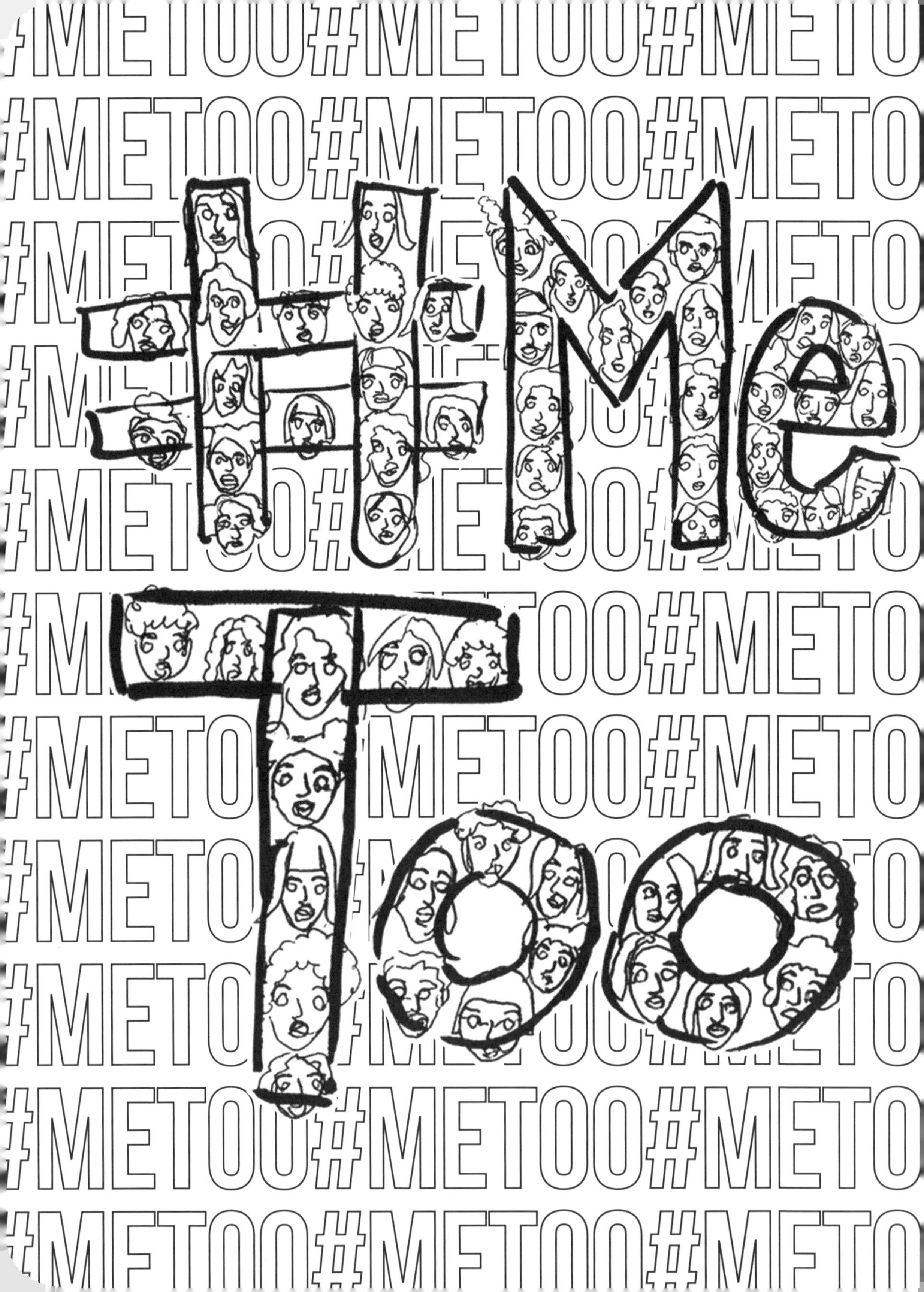
#MeToo

FEBRUARY

VIOLENCE PREVENTION MONTH

M	T	W	T	F	S	S
				1	2	3
4	5	6	7	8	9	10
11	12	13	14	15	16	17
18	19	20	21	22	23	24
25	26	27	28	1	2	3

31 THURSDAY

1 FRIDAY

2 SATURDAY

Groundhog Day

3 SUNDAY

THOUGHTS AND INSPIRATION

FEBRUARY

VIOLENCE PREVENTION MONTH

M	T	W	T	F	S	S
				1	2	3
4	5	6	7	8	9	10
11	12	13	14	15	16	17
18	19	20	21	22	23	24
25	26	27	28	1	2	3

4 MONDAY

5 TUESDAY

Chinese New Year

6 WEDNESDAY

THINGS TO DO

WEEKLY GOALS AND NOTES

7 THURSDAY

8 FRIDAY

9 SATURDAY

10 SUNDAY

THOUGHTS AND INSPIRATION

FEBRUARY

VIOLENCE PREVENTION MONTH

M	T	W	T	F	S	S
				1	2	3
4	5	6	7	8	9	10
11	12	13	14	15	16	17
18	19	20	21	22	23	24
25	26	27	28	1	2	3

11 MONDAY

12 TUESDAY

13 WEDNESDAY

THINGS TO DO

WEEKLY GOALS AND NOTES

14 THURSDAY

Valentine's Day

15 FRIDAY

16 SATURDAY

17 SUNDAY

THOUGHTS AND INSPIRATION

FEBRUARY

VIOLENCE PREVENTION MONTH

M	T	W	T	F	S	S
				1	2	3
4	5	6	7	8	9	10
11	12	13	14	15	16	17
18	19	20	21	22	23	24
25	26	27	28	1	2	3

18 MONDAY

19 TUESDAY

20 WEDNESDAY

THINGS TO DO

WEEKLY GOALS AND NOTES

21 THURSDAY

22 FRIDAY

23 SATURDAY

24 SUNDAY

THOUGHTS AND INSPIRATION

FEBRUARY

VIOLENCE PREVENTION MONTH

M	T	W	T	F	S	S
				1	2	3
4	5	6	7	8	9	10
11	12	13	14	15	16	17
18	19	20	21	22	23	24
25	26	27	28	1	2	3

25 MONDAY

26 TUESDAY

27 WEDNESDAY

THINGS TO DO

WEEKLY GOALS AND NOTES

28 THURSDAY

FEBRUARY 26–MARCH 4 **NATIONAL EATING DISORDERS AWARENESS WEEK**

MARCH

FOCUS ON
ONE OF YOUR
STRENGTHS

CIRCLE ONE

I'm woke!

Having feelings

I'm awesome!

Idea crush

Fuck the patriarchy!

Did I self-care?

MONDAY	TUESDAY	WEDNESDAY
4	5	6
11	12	13
18	19	20
25	26	27

WHAT HAVE YOU DONE FOR SELF-CARE THIS MONTH?

#FEMINISTFRIDAY
PAY IT FORWARD

HOW DID YOU RESIST?

THURSDAY	FRIDAY	SATURDAY	SUNDAY
	1	2	3
7	8	9	10
14	15	16	17
21	22	23	24
28	29	30	31

NOTES

#LETHER WORK

Heather Gillis

This past year I found myself in the news instead of writing it.

A man yelled FHRITP at me from a passing truck in April 2017 as I finished an interview at the landfill in St. John's.

I had had enough. The phrase has been yelled at me multiple times. And at nearly all of my colleagues, at all media outlets, regardless of gender.

Each time this phrase is hurled, it's an attempt to sabotage our work, our interviews, and our live shots.

So I tweeted a photo of that truck. It went viral. It had more than 84,000 views, nearly 14,000 engagements, and was trending in Canada.

The police weighed in on Twitter. They said they could investigate. I filed a complaint. The man was charged under the criminal code with causing a disturbance. The case went to trial. A judge dismissed it. He said, in this case, there was no disturbance because the use or operation of the landfill wasn't impacted.

The decision got a lot of media attention. It's because it has implications for working reporters across the country, especially women.

While the initial incident and court decision were disappointing, the aftermath and online trolling was troubling.

Keyboard warriors have sought out my email writing that if I have FHRITP yelled at me so often, "Maybe, you deserve it?"

Another troll wrote calling me a tart, saying I was hired for my looks, and that I shouldn't bitch about being treated like one.

I have two university degrees, and a couple of journalism awards to my name–things you only earn with hard work. I'm no tart, baby.

But that's not the worst part. Every woman at my station who has a photo on the website, has been targeted with anonymous letters, allegedly from British Columbia. They say FHRITP. And I feel like it's my fault that my fellow female colleagues have been targeted. It's because I spoke up, and said it wasn't okay.

I never dreamed a tweet and a photo would land me in court, or as a keynote speaker at a conference talking about harassment that female journalists face, or in the news instead of on it.

There have been a slew of people, all men, charged for yelling FHRITP at reporters since my case.

Misogyny and disrespect are at the core of the phrase. And it perpetuates rape culture.

Still, I'm not alone in wanting to work unencumbered. Female sports reporters in Brazil have launched a campaign detailing the harassment they face on the job called "Let Her Work." And I couldn't agree more. No matter the occupation.

Heather Gillis is a reporter at NTV News and is the co-host of the NTV Sunday Evening Newshour. She joined NTV in 2011 after completing a Bachelor of Journalism at the University of King's College in Halifax, and a Bachelor of Arts at Memorial University. Gillis is a competitive rower in the Royal St. John's Regatta, and a former dancer completing ballet exams at the Advanced level.

Alick Tsui Photography

MARCH

M	T	W	T	F	S	S
				1	2	3
4	5	6	7	8	9	10
11	12	13	14	15	16	17
18	19	20	21	22	23	24
25	26	27	28	29	30	31

28 THURSDAY

1 FRIDAY

Self-injury Awareness Day

2 SATURDAY

3 SUNDAY

International Sex Workers' Rights Day

THOUGHTS AND INSPIRATION

MARCH

M	T	W	T	F	S	S
				1	2	3
4	5	6	7	8	9	10
11	12	13	14	15	16	17
18	19	20	21	22	23	24
25	26	27	28	29	30	31

4 MONDAY

Maha Shivratri

5 TUESDAY

Shrove Tuesday (Pancake Day)

#NLHISTORY Demasduit (1796-1820), a Beothuk woman, was captured on this date in 1819 by Bay of Exploits planters John Peyton, his son John Jr., and their party. Demasduit's husband, Nonosbawsut, was shot and killed when he attempted to rescue his wife from Peyton.

6 WEDNESDAY

Ash Wednesday

THINGS TO DO

WEEKLY GOALS AND NOTES

7 THURSDAY

8 FRIDAY

International Women's Day

9 SATURDAY

10 SUNDAY

Daylight Savings Time Begins

THOUGHTS AND INSPIRATION

MARCH

M	T	W	T	F	S	S
				1	2	3
4	5	6	7	8	9	10
11	12	13	14	15	16	17
18	19	20	21	22	23	24
25	26	27	28	29	30	31

11 MONDAY

Commonwealth Day

12 TUESDAY

13 WEDNESDAY

THINGS TO DO

WEEKLY GOALS AND NOTES

14 THURSDAY

15 FRIDAY

16 SATURDAY

17 SUNDAY

St. Patrick's Day

THOUGHTS AND INSPIRATION

MARCH

M	T	W	T	F	S	S
				1	2	3
4	5	6	7	8	9	10
11	12	13	14	15	16	17
18	19	20	21	22	23	24
25	26	27	28	29	30	31

18 MONDAY

19 TUESDAY

20 WEDNESDAY

Purim
Holi Begins
Equinox
First Day of Spring

THINGS TO DO

WEEKLY GOALS AND NOTES

21 THURSDAY

Holi Ends

22 FRIDAY

23 SATURDAY

24 SUNDAY

THOUGHTS AND INSPIRATION

MARCH

M	T	W	T	F	S	S
				1	2	3
4	5	6	7	8	9	10
11	12	13	14	15	16	17
18	19	20	21	22	23	24
25	26	27	28	29	30	31

25 MONDAY

26 TUESDAY

27 WEDNESDAY

THINGS TO DO

WEEKLY GOALS AND NOTES

28 THURSDAY

29 FRIDAY

30 SATURDAY

31 SUNDAY

THOUGHTS AND INSPIRATION

BEER IS AMAZING

Alicia MacDonald and Christina Coady

Beer is amazing. It can be a culinary pursuit, the drive behind vibrant small business, a tourism icon, a community-building beverage, and something that is increasingly becoming a diverse and exciting industry in this province. With the craft-beer industry taking off in Newfoundland, with more and more women both in the industry and enjoying brews than ever before, there is no better time to get acquainted with beer. In fact, here are just a few reasons to get you excited about drinking beer.

Beer and its incredible variety of styles offers an endless plethora of flavours. Beers can be described as light, citrusy, sweet, bitter, sour, or funky to name a few. Flavour profiles can include lemon zest, melon, stone fruit, earthy, or spicy, among many other profiles. It's best to start with what you know and already love. If you love crisp and tangy white wines, you may enjoy sour beers that are generously hopped to bring out beautiful fruit flavours. Enjoy rich and bold coffee flavours? There are many stouts and porters brewed locally that will suit your tastes!

Beer, especially independent craft beer, lends itself to a world of flavours and adventure. Beer travel is rising in popularity where couples, groups, or families travel to beer destinations such as Belgium, New England, or smaller and more unique rural locations. Its complexity also pairs perfectly with active lifestyles and is a great way to celebrate the fact you just put up your tent in record time, completed a hard bike ride or epic trail hike, or wrapped up a beautiful yoga session.

Craft beer is also a community that is growing as quickly as its industry. Visiting cozy taprooms at local breweries is an excellent way to become a part of this community! You can try exciting beers, meet new people, and learn about your local brewery. This also extends to events, tour groups, online educational groups, and social groups that all create welcoming spaces to meet others and try beers. A special way that women can get involved in the local craft-beer community is to join the Newfoundland women's beer collective, called the Brewnettes. All women are welcome to join, regardless of their beer experience. Members get together once a month to enjoy craft beer and it's a great way to learn, share knowledge, and have fun with unique beer as well as meet new friends.

With all the new breweries opening around Newfoundland and Labrador, there has never been a better time to pick up a new brew and fall in love with beer. Grab a friend or loved one, pop down to your local brewery's taproom, and try a new beer together!

Alicia MacDonald is the co-owner and head brewer at Port Rexton Brewing. After brewing and training with NS breweries, she moved from her hometown of Truro, NS, to Newfoundland in 2015 to start the Port Rexton Brewing Co. with her Clarenville-born wife.

Christina Coady is co-owner and head brewer at Landwash Brewery in Mount Pearl, Newfoundland. She was the co-head brewer at Folly Brewpub in Toronto, Ontario, for three years before moving back home to St. John's with her partner to build Landwash Brewery.

APRIL

FOCUS ON ONE OF YOUR STRENGTHS

CIRCLE ONE

I'm woke!

Having feelings

I'm awesome!

Idea crush

Fuck the patriarchy!

Did I self-care?

MONDAY	TUESDAY	WEDNESDAY
1	2	3
8	8	10
15	16	17
22	23	24
29	30	

WHAT HAVE YOU DONE FOR SELF-CARE THIS MONTH?

#FEMINISTFRIDAY
PAY IT FORWARD

HOW DID YOU RESIST?

THURSDAY	FRIDAY	SATURDAY	SUNDAY
4	5	6	7
11	12	13	14
18	19	20	21
25	26	27	28

NOTES

APRIL

M	T	W	T	F	S	S
1	2	3	4	5	6	7
8	9	10	11	12	13	14
15	16	17	18	19	20	21
22	23	24	25	26	27	28
29	30	1	2	3	4	5

1 MONDAY

April Fool's Day

2 TUESDAY

3 WEDNESDAY

THINGS TO DO

WEEKLY GOALS AND NOTES

4 THURSDAY

#NLHISTORY In 1933, Louise Maud Saunders is called to the Bar, becoming Newfoundland's first female lawyer.

5 FRIDAY

6 SATURDAY

7 SUNDAY

THOUGHTS AND INSPIRATION

APRIL

M	T	W	T	F	S	S
1	2	3	4	5	6	7
8	9	10	11	12	13	14
15	16	17	18	19	20	21
22	23	24	25	26	27	28
29	30	1	2	3	4	5

8 MONDAY

9 TUESDAY

Vimy Ridge Day

10 WEDNESDAY

THINGS TO DO

WEEKLY GOALS AND NOTES

11 THURSDAY

12 FRIDAY

13 SATURDAY

#NLHISTORY In 1925, suffragists in Newfoundland and Labrador gained the right to vote and to serve as elected representatives.

14 SUNDAY

Palm Sunday
Rama Navami

THOUGHTS AND INSPIRATION

APRIL

APRIL 15–21 **NATIONAL VOLUNTEER WEEK**

M	T	W	T	F	S	S
1	2	3	4	5	6	7
8	9	10	11	12	13	14
15	16	17	18	19	20	21
22	23	24	25	26	27	28
29	30	1	2	3	4	5

15 MONDAY

16 TUESDAY

17 WEDNESDAY

THINGS TO DO

WEEKLY GOALS AND NOTES

18 THURSDAY

Maundy Thursday

19 FRIDAY

Good Friday
First Day of Passover

20 SATURDAY

21 SUNDAY

Easter Sunday

THOUGHTS AND INSPIRATION

APRIL

M	T	W	T	F	S	S
1	2	3	4	5	6	7
8	9	10	11	12	13	14
15	16	17	18	19	20	21
22	23	24	25	26	27	28
29	30	1	2	3	4	5

22 MONDAY

Easter Monday

23 TUESDAY

St. George's Day

24 WEDNESDAY

THINGS TO DO

WEEKLY GOALS AND NOTES

25 THURSDAY

26 FRIDAY

27 SATURDAY

Last Day of Passover

28 SUNDAY

THOUGHTS AND INSPIRATION

APRIL

M	T	W	T	F	S	S
1	2	3	4	5	6	7
8	9	10	11	12	13	14
15	16	17	18	19	20	21
22	23	24	25	26	27	28
29	30	1	2	3	4	5

29 MONDAY

30 TUESDAY

NOTES

WHAT FEMINISM IS TO ME

Raylene Noftall

When women no longer fear rape or beatings from a spouse
And when women no longer feel it's their duty to clean the house
When women can walk the streets without having to look behind their back
And when women can live one day without being sexualized on every magazine rack
This is what feminism is to me...
When women can enter any classroom and not feel a hostile chill
And when women can receive a paycheck to cover all of the bills
When women can work a job and not come home to start another
And every time a child is sick the first one to call is Mother
This is what feminism is to me...
When young girls can have a good time without being objectified and harassed
And when women at work don't get a sexy smirk every time they pass
When women are free of stereotypes and the world is colour blind
And when theory isn't occupying every woman's mind
This is what feminism is to me...
We have to put our lives into perspective and ask the question "why"?
You search for the answers but it all begins with "I"
The key to change is to start with your life first
Then you will shortly see...
The personal is political, that's what feminism is to me.

Raylene Noftall joined the St. John's Status of Women Council team as Program Coordinator of Marguerite's Place in April 2017. Raylene graduated with a Master of Social Work degree from Barry University, Miami, Florida in 2011. Raylene has practiced social work internationally but is most passionate about community based, grassroots social-work approaches. Raylene is a real-life energizer bunny, and when she is not advocating and demanding social change she can be found tending bar, or hiking.

FEMINIST HASHTAG ROUND-UP

We are more interconnected globally than ever before, with social media platforms allowing us to learn from each other and support each other's feminist struggles, shout-outs, and successes across cities, provinces, and countries. From trans women's representations to migrant justice to survivors of sexual violence showing up for each other, hashtags continue to broaden our feminist movement. Here is our feminist hashtag round-up, highlighting our favourite, fierce, feminist conversations, clapbacks, campaigns, and causes.

#REFUGEESWELCOME

#TIMESUP

#IllRideWithYou

#CRIPTHEVOTE

#LOVEYOURLINES

#ShoutYourStatus

#DisabledAndCute

#FREETHENIPPLE

#MuslimWomensDay

#IWD2018

#SEXWORKISWORK

#TogetherWeRise

#PAYUPNL

#NASTYWOMEN

#WhyIMarch

#RAPECULTUREISWHEN

#HUMANRIGHTS

#ImWithHer

#SHEINSPIRESME

#FEMINISTFRIDAY

#NLWomenRising

#EffYourBeautyStandards

#BRINGBACKOURGIRLS

#YouOKSis

#RightsNotRescue

#MMIWG

WHAT ARE YOUR FAVOURITE HASHTAGS?

MAY

FOCUS ON ONE OF YOUR STRENGTHS

CIRCLE ONE

I'm woke!

Having feelings

I'm awesome!

Idea crush

Fuck the patriarchy!

Did I self-care?

MONDAY	TUESDAY	WEDNESDAY
		1
6	7	8
13	14	15
20	21	22
27	28	29

WHAT HAVE YOU DONE FOR SELF-CARE THIS MONTH?

#FEMINISTFRIDAY
PAY IT FORWARD

HOW DID YOU RESIST?

THURSDAY	FRIDAY	SATURDAY	SUNDAY
2	3	4	5
9	10	11	12
16	17	18	19
23	24	25	26
30	31		

NOTES

MAY

M	T	W	T	F	S	S
		1	2	3	4	5
6	7	8	9	10	11	12
13	14	15	16	17	18	19
20	21	22	23	24	25	26
27	28	29	30	31	1	2

29 MONDAY

30 TUESDAY

1 WEDNESDAY

May Day

THINGS TO DO

WEEKLY GOALS AND NOTES

2 THURSDAY

3 FRIDAY

4 SATURDAY

5 SUNDAY

International Midwifery Day
Ramadan Begins

THOUGHTS AND INSPIRATION

MAY

M	T	W	T	F	S	S
		1	2	3	4	5
6	7	8	9	10	11	12
13	14	15	16	17	18	19
20	21	22	23	24	25	26
27	28	29	30	31	1	2

6 MONDAY

7 TUESDAY

8 WEDNESDAY

THINGS TO DO

WEEKLY GOALS AND NOTES

9 THURSDAY

10 FRIDAY

11 SATURDAY

12 SUNDAY

Mother's Day

THOUGHTS AND INSPIRATION

MAY

M	T	W	T	F	S	S
		1	2	3	4	5
6	7	8	9	10	11	12
13	14	15	16	17	18	19
20	21	22	23	24	25	26
27	28	29	30	31	1	2

13 MONDAY

14 TUESDAY

15 WEDNESDAY

THINGS TO DO

WEEKLY GOALS AND NOTES

16 THURSDAY

17 FRIDAY

International Day against Homophobia, Transphobia, and Biphobia

#NLHISTORY On this day in 1930, Lady Helena E. Squires became the first woman to hold a seat in the Newfoundland and Labrador House of Assembly.

18 SATURDAY

19 SUNDAY

THOUGHTS AND INSPIRATION

MAY

M	T	W	T	F	S	S
		1	2	3	4	5
6	7	8	9	10	11	12
13	14	15	16	17	18	19
20	21	22	23	24	25	26
27	28	29	30	31	1	2

20 MONDAY

Victoria Day

21 TUESDAY

22 WEDNESDAY

THINGS TO DO

WEEKLY GOALS AND NOTES

23 THURSDAY

24 FRIDAY

25 SATURDAY

26 SUNDAY

THOUGHTS AND INSPIRATION

MAY

M	T	W	T	F	S	S
		1	2	3	4	5
6	7	8	9	10	11	12
13	14	15	16	17	18	19
20	21	22	23	24	25	26
27	28	29	30	31	1	2

27 MONDAY

28 TUESDAY

29 WEDNESDAY

THINGS TO DO

WEEKLY GOALS AND NOTES

30 THURSDAY

31 FRIDAY

GIRLS JUST WANNA HAVE FUNDAMENTAL HUMAN RIGHTS

WHEN YOUR PARTNER DECIDES THE DEAL IS OFF AND YOU'RE SCREWED

Kelly Knee

My war had begun, and I had no idea I was about to be standing right in the middle, with all ammunition pointing at me. It was a war I thought I would lose, but every time I was hit, I rose back up and became stronger each time, until finally it ended, and I was a woman I never dreamed I could ever be. A woman that fought with everything I had in me and became self-reliant because I knew if there was anybody I could count on, it was going to be myself.

Infidelity! Infidelity eleven years after I had made a verbal agreement between myself and my husband that, because I was the mother, I would be the stay-at-home parent and he would be the breadwinner. We still considered each other as equals, only I wouldn't be making the money. That lasted for eleven years, and then he decided, after I finished my breast-cancer treatment, the deal was off. I was screwed!

What was I to do? How could he leave me? How can I make it on my own? I have no work experience! I have no money! I have five kids and no money! The panic set in, and I begged him to stay because I couldn't survive this world without him. I was already depressed and didn't know it. My breast-cancer diagnosis did a number on me, but him leaving me in this world alone with our children caused me to have a mental breakdown. I believed there was no coming back from all this devastation.

One day, out of nowhere, I decided I had to fight, if not for myself, for my children. If cancer couldn't bring me down, I'd be damned if I'd let this man destroy me. Halfway through my war, right at the peak of it, he tried to take it all from me. He wanted to stop all support payments, and he wanted the children and I evicted from our family home. That's when I knew I had to fight – not only for myself, but for every woman out there that has ever felt trapped, thinking they couldn't make it on their own without their husband. I had a lawyer, and I faced my ex in court, and to my delight, the judge practically laughed in his face. There is no such thing as "the deal is off and I'm screwed." I rose above every roadblock and fought for everything I have. I starting blogging about my experiences, both physical and emotional, hoping to reach at least one person who thought they could never leave because they couldn't live without their partner. Well, I'm here again to tell you that you can. You are not screwed.

I am a stay-at-home, single mother of five boys, four years cancer free, divorced, running a home business, and a volunteer Localife Leader with YACC (Young Adult Cancer Canada). There are days that are hard, but I am not screwed. I can do this…I am doing this!

Kelly is a four-year breast cancer survivor, divorced, single stay-at-home mother of five handsome boys, international blogger on her journey with cancer and beyond, volunteer Localife Leader with YACC (Young Adult Cancer Canada) and owner of a web-based business selling unique, one-of-a-kind, sea-glass jewellery and designs.

JUNE

FOCUS ON ONE OF YOUR STRENGTHS

CIRCLE ONE

I'm woke!

Having feelings

I'm awesome!

Idea crush

Fuck the patriarchy!

Did I self-care?

MONDAY	TUESDAY	WEDNESDAY
3	4	5
10	11	12
17	18	19
24	25	26

WHAT HAVE YOU DONE FOR SELF-CARE THIS MONTH?

#FEMINISTFRIDAY
PAY IT FORWARD

HOW DID YOU RESIST?

THURSDAY	FRIDAY	SATURDAY	SUNDAY
		1	2
6	7	8	9
13	14	15	16
20	21	22	23
27	28	29	30

NOTES

Sex workers are best kind

JUNE

M	T	W	T	F	S	S
					1	2
3	4	5	6	7	8	9
10	11	12	13	14	15	16
17	18	19	20	21	22	23
24	25	26	27	28	29	30

30 THURSDAY

31 FRIDAY

1 SATURDAY

2 SUNDAY

International Sex Workers' Day | International Whores' Day

THOUGHTS AND INSPIRATION

JUNE

M	T	W	T	F	S	S
					1	2
3	4	5	6	7	8	9
10	11	12	13	14	15	16
17	18	19	20	21	22	23
24	25	26	27	28	29	30

3 MONDAY

4 TUESDAY

Ramadan Ends
Eid al-Fitr Begins at Sundown

5 WEDNESDAY

Eid al-Fitr

THINGS TO DO

WEEKLY GOALS AND NOTES

6 THURSDAY

7 FRIDAY

8 SATURDAY

9 SUNDAY

THOUGHTS AND INSPIRATION

JUNE

M	T	W	T	F	S	S
					1	2
3	4	5	6	7	8	9
10	11	12	13	14	15	16
17	18	19	20	21	22	23
24	25	26	27	28	29	30

10 MONDAY

11 TUESDAY

12 WEDNESDAY

THINGS TO DO

WEEKLY GOALS AND NOTES

13 THURSDAY

14 FRIDAY

National Day of Action for Sex Workers' Rights

#NLHISTORY On this day in 2015, the first ever St. John's Slutwalk was held.

15 SATURDAY

Elder Abuse Awareness Day

16 SUNDAY

Father's Day
International Domestic Workers' Day

THOUGHTS AND INSPIRATION

JUNE

M	T	W	T	F	S	S
					1	2
3	4	5	6	7	8	9
10	11	12	13	14	15	16
17	18	19	20	21	22	23
24	25	26	27	28	29	30

17 MONDAY

18 TUESDAY

19 WEDNESDAY

THINGS TO DO

WEEKLY GOALS AND NOTES

20 THURSDAY

21 FRIDAY

National Indigenous Peoples Day
Summer Solstice | First day of Summer

22 SATURDAY

23 SUNDAY

THOUGHTS AND INSPIRATION

JUNE

M	T	W	T	F	S	S
					1	2
3	4	5	6	7	8	9
10	11	12	13	14	15	16
17	18	19	20	21	22	23
24	25	26	27	28	29	30

24 MONDAY

25 TUESDAY

#NLHISTORY Newfoundland Status of Women Council bought their first home in 1987 on Military Road.

26 WEDNESDAY

THINGS TO DO

WEEKLY GOALS AND NOTES

27 THURSDAY

Multiculturalism Day

28 FRIDAY

29 SATURDAY

30 SUNDAY

THOUGHTS AND INSPIRATION

fem [FIVE]

TOP FIVE WAYS TO
ENGAGE IN "THE FISHERY"

Kimberly Orren

In Newfoundland & Labrador, only about 20% of those who fish commercially or recreationally are women, and even fewer are engaged in leadership roles. Yet, we often describe ourselves – aboriginal or settler – as a Sea People. Whether we think about fish as food or commodity, or fishing as an activity of our culture, women have little say in how it is being utilized and prosecuted. It is time for us to move from the shore and take a place in the boat – and the boardroom!

[1] EXPAND YOUR VIEW OF "THE FISHERY."

For generations, more than 80% of us were involved in summer cod fishing as a livelihood and a rich culture developed over the long winter! Songs and stories of fishing and adventures on the sea – even hooked rugs of boats and harbour scenes. But now less than 2% of us fish commercially, and even the numbers of us who fish recreationally, whether for cod or trout or salmon, is decreasing! Get a fishing pole or hand reel, and go fishing! Whatever the fish, make it your fishery.

[2] RE-DISCOVER YOUR FAMILY/CULTURE'S FISHING STORIES.

From human pre-history, we have fished – every culture has stories of fishing whether from ponds, lakes, rivers, or the mighty ocean – humans have depended upon protein from the sea! Little dried fish fed those who built the pyramids of Egypt and the fishing flakes of Newfoundland & Labrador! Ask your family for their stories and recipes and songs about fishing - no matter where you were knit, there are stories. Or connect with someone new by asking them about their fishing tales!

[3] BE INSPIRED.

Let fishing be your muse! Paint the tall tales of fishing onto your canvas or carve them into your sculpture. Or learn a fishing skill and use it as another medium in your work. For example, the same skill to knit twine into net can be used to knit a scarf or learn to weave rope. Working rope and twine is one of the most ancient of skills and placing it in your artist's tool box helps to keep these skills alive, ensuring that fishing will always be a part of our human story.

[4] SUPPORT LOCAL FOOD.

Newfoundland & Labrador is highly dependent upon imported food. Play a part in changing this and buy local food, especially fish! Part of the story of fishing is fish as our cultural food. Eat more local fish; ask for it where you shop; and introduce your children to fish! There's more than "fee & chee;" reclaim your cultural food and reinvigorate it with recipes from around the world!

[5] GET IN THE BOAT.

THIS is the hard part! It's no good to just call for equity. We have to work at it! It's not good enough to encourage our daughters to be brave if we aren't leading by example. As women we have been conditioned to let the man drive the boat, bait the hook, and take off the fish! And I'm talking about more than fishing. Some of the most exciting experiences in our lives, at play and work – we have just been spectators. Lean in – jump in – participate in your own life! Confidence in outdoor activities is empowering and you may just find yourself taking the lead at work, too. Be a champion – educate yourself about the issues – get involved in consultation processes – let your voice be heard! Start your training to get in the boat–get your Pleasure Craft Operator Card and keep going! Then one day you'll find that there are more women in the boat, maybe as professional fish harvesters, and serving as corporate seafood executives!

Kimberly is co-founder and volunteer project manager for Fishing for Success in Petty Harbour, NL. She is a former high-school science teacher with a passion for fishing. When she saw the need to reconnect youth with their fishing heritage, she went back to graduate school to study Fisheries and Aquatic Sciences. Kimberly has since become a NL hunting and fishing guide, boat captain, and is working towards earning a commercial fishing license. She was recently recognized by YWCA St John's as a 2018 Women of Distinction in Mentorship & Education for her work with the Girls Who Fish and Youth Cod Fishery programs.

Photo by Megan Meadus

JULY

FOCUS ON ONE OF YOUR STRENGTHS

CIRCLE ONE

I'm woke!

Having feelings

I'm awesome!

Idea crush

Fuck the patriarchy!

Did I self-care?

MONDAY	TUESDAY	WEDNESDAY
1	2	3
8	8	10
15	16	17
22	23	24
29	30	31

WHAT HAVE YOU DONE FOR SELF-CARE THIS MONTH?

#FEMINISTFRIDAY

PAY IT FORWARD

HOW DID YOU RESIST?

THURSDAY	FRIDAY	SATURDAY	SUNDAY
4	5	6	7
11	12	13	14
18	19	20	21
25	26	27	28

NOTES

JULY

M	T	W	T	F	S	S
1	2	3	4	5	6	7
8	9	10	11	12	13	14
15	16	17	18	19	20	21
22	23	24	25	26	27	28
29	30	31	1	2	3	4

1 MONDAY

Canada Day | Memorial Day in Newfoundland and Labrador

2 TUESDAY

3 WEDNESDAY

THINGS TO DO

WEEKLY GOALS AND NOTES

4 THURSDAY

5 FRIDAY

6 SATURDAY

7 SUNDAY

THOUGHTS AND INSPIRATION

JULY

M	T	W	T	F	S	S
1	2	3	4	5	6	7
8	9	10	11	12	13	14
15	16	17	18	19	20	21
22	23	24	25	26	27	28
29	30	31	1	2	3	4

8 MONDAY

9 TUESDAY

10 WEDNESDAY

THINGS TO DO

WEEKLY GOALS AND NOTES

11 THURSDAY

12 FRIDAY

Orangemen's Day

13 SATURDAY

14 SUNDAY

THOUGHTS AND INSPIRATION

JULY

M	T	W	T	F	S	S
1	2	3	4	5	6	7
8	9	10	11	12	13	14
15	16	17	18	19	20	21
22	23	24	25	26	27	28
29	30	31	1	2	3	4

15 MONDAY

16 TUESDAY

17 WEDNESDAY

THINGS TO DO

WEEKLY GOALS AND NOTES

18 THURSDAY

19 FRIDAY

20 SATURDAY

21 SUNDAY

THOUGHTS AND INSPIRATION

JULY

M	T	W	T	F	S	S
1	2	3	4	5	6	7
8	9	10	11	12	13	14
15	16	17	18	19	20	21
22	23	24	25	26	27	28
29	30	31	1	2	3	4

22 MONDAY

23 TUESDAY

24 WEDNESDAY

THINGS TO DO

WEEKLY GOALS AND NOTES

25 THURSDAY

26 FRIDAY

27 SATURDAY

28 SUNDAY

THOUGHTS AND INSPIRATION

JULY

M	T	W	T	F	S	S
1	2	3	4	5	6	7
8	9	10	11	12	13	14
15	16	17	18	19	20	21
22	23	24	25	26	27	28
29	30	31	1	2	3	4

29 MONDAY

30 TUESDAY

31 WEDNESDAY

THINGS TO DO

SPACE OF INFINITE POSSIBILTY

#ENOUGH

Dwan Street

"I'm some glad I don't work in the office with you."

"Why?"

"Because you'd be saying, 'Me too.'"

If I were to describe the surge of rage I felt when a man leaned in and said those words to me in a meeting, I might need all the pages of this edition. Yes b'y, sexual assault jokes are hilarious. Sit your ass down.

I was infuriated. And, as I sat seething, NTV's Heather Gillis was sitting in a courtroom. She was bravely facing the "man" (I use that term loosely) who had yelled, "Fuck her right in the pussy," as she was working, interviewing the city's mayor.

Then, the judge ruled there had been no criminal offence. While I am no student of the law, I joined the countless number of people who wondered, "How?" and exclaimed simultaneously, "Enough."

I work in a male-dominated industry, but fortunately in a workplace with zero tolerance for harassment. Does this mean my days are void of the bullshit some folks believe is okay behaviour? No.

I have been told there will be "bloodshed" in a meeting by a man who was spitting in my face.

I have had a fist cocked in my face and called a "cunt" while explaining policy.

I have been asked in a meeting if I was "there to cook dinner."

I have had advances made to grab my crotch when I walk by to get a coffee.

The list is not limited there.

Here is a newsflash: THIS IS NOT OKAY, B'YS. NOT. OKAY.

We know now that even our own legislature is not void of these behaviours, and that is both disheartening and infuriating.

Heather Gillis, you, I, every human being – all have a right to go to work, feel safe, and do our jobs. We deserve to continue through our days feeling accomplished; not violated, disrespected, and unvalued.

Our little girls, young women, and fellow women deserve to live without this type of bullshit – threats, violence, the lump in your throat when afraid to speak up, and the fear that makes us walk to our cars from our workplaces with keys placed strategically between our fingers.

Our little boys, young men, and men need to say this is not okay. We know our allies are out there. We see you, raising your sons to be strong men who build women up and do not trivialize their existence down to something for sex and pleasure.

Let us do our jobs, and just be decent people. Carry that message beyond your workplace and into every day.

I'm still angry. You should be too.

Let's harness that power and be the engine for change.

Dwan Street grew up in the small fishing community of Spillar's Cove, Newfoundland and Labrador, and comes from a long line of fish harvesters and fish processing workers. Growing up in a fishing household meant knowing the importance of a strong union that fights for workers' rights and social justice. She joined FFAW-Unifor in 2014.

Dwan holds a BA (Sociology and Anthropology), MA (Social Anthropology), and Master of Marine Studies (Fisheries Resource Management). She is a proud feminist and Board member of the St. John's Status of Women Council. She also serves on the Executive of Unifor's Atlantic Regional Council, as well as Unifor's National Fisheries Industry Council. Dwan also serves on the Board of the Canadian Independent Fish Harvester Federation.

In her spare time, Dwan is a triathlete, runner, and hockey player, and continues to promote the importance of strength and healthy body image for women and girls in all levels of sport.

AUGUST

FOCUS ON ONE OF YOUR STRENGTHS

CIRCLE ONE

I'm woke!

Having feelings

I'm awesome!

Idea crush

Fuck the patriarchy!

Did I self-care?

MONDAY	TUESDAY	WEDNESDAY
5	6	7
12	13	14
19	20	21
26	27	28

WHAT HAVE YOU DONE FOR SELF-CARE THIS MONTH?

#FEMINISTFRIDAY
PAY IT FORWARD

HOW DID YOU RESIST?

THURSDAY	FRIDAY	SATURDAY	SUNDAY
1	2	3	4
8	9	10	11
15	16	17	18
22	23	24	25
29	30	31	

NOTES

I don't want flowers,
I want equal pay

AUGUST

M	T	W	T	F	S	S
			1	2	3	4
5	6	7	8	9	10	11
12	13	14	15	16	17	18
19	20	21	22	23	24	25
26	27	28	29	30	31	1

1 THURSDAY

2 FRIDAY

3 SATURDAY

4 SUNDAY

THOUGHTS AND INSPIRATION

AUGUST

M	T	W	T	F	S	S
			1	2	3	4
5	6	7	8	9	10	11
12	13	14	15	16	17	18
19	20	21	22	23	24	25
26	27	28	29	30	31	1

5 MONDAY

6 TUESDAY

7 WEDNESDAY

Regatta Day

THINGS TO DO

WEEKLY GOALS AND NOTES

8 THURSDAY

9 FRIDAY

10 SATURDAY

Prisoners' Justice Day

#NLHISTORY On this day in 1947, Phyllis (Penney) Gaul, Newfoundland's first female pilot, received her pilot's licence.

11 SUNDAY

THOUGHTS AND INSPIRATION

AUGUST

M	T	W	T	F	S	S
			1	2	3	4
5	6	7	8	9	10	11
12	13	14	15	16	17	18
19	20	21	22	23	24	25
26	27	28	29	30	31	1

12 MONDAY

13 TUESDAY

#NLHISTORY On this day in 1856, the first record of women rowing in the Royal St. John's Regatta took place.

14 WEDNESDAY

THINGS TO DO

WEEKLY GOALS AND NOTES

15 THURSDAY

16 FRIDAY

17 SATURDAY

18 SUNDAY

THOUGHTS AND INSPIRATION

AUGUST

M	T	W	T	F	S	S
			1	2	3	4
5	6	7	8	9	10	11
12	13	14	15	16	17	18
19	20	21	22	23	24	25
26	27	28	29	30	31	1

19 MONDAY

20 TUESDAY

21 WEDNESDAY

THINGS TO DO

WEEKLY GOALS AND NOTES

22 THURSDAY

23 FRIDAY

24 SATURDAY

Krishna Janmashtami

25 SUNDAY

#NLHISTORY On this day in 2016, the first ever FemFestNL kicked off in St. John's.

THOUGHTS AND INSPIRATION

AUGUST

M	T	W	T	F	S	S
			1	2	3	4
5	6	7	8	9	10	11
12	13	14	15	16	17	18
19	20	21	22	23	24	25
26	27	28	29	30	31	1

26 MONDAY

27 TUESDAY

28 WEDNESDAY

THINGS TO DO

WEEKLY GOALS AND NOTES

29 THURSDAY

30 FRIDAY

31 SATURDAY

SEPTEMBER

1 SUNDAY

Muharram | Islamic New Year

THOUGHTS AND INSPIRATION

fem [FIVE]

FIVE TIPS FOR
SURVIVING AND THRIVING
IN A MALE-DOMINATED FIELD OF WORK

Alanna Husch

The recent #MeToo movement has brought to light a lot of inequalities that many women face in their workplaces, as well as in some cases harassment and even assault. I am in the minority in Canada, with only approximately 15% of orthopedic surgeons identifying as women in Canadian hospitals. And while I was fortunate to have been well supported throughout my training, I have also adopted some skills that have allowed me to thrive in a male-dominated workplace.

[1] PLAY TO YOUR STRENGTHS.

I find myself to be an effective communicator in times of stress, particularly with patients who may be having the worst day of their life. Empathy, compassion, and kindness come easier to me than to some of my male colleagues. We all have strengths and weaknesses, and sitting down to remember your strengths and continue developing them will allow you success in any field.

[2] CHALLENGE TRADITIONAL GENDER ROLES.

This doesn't necessarily mean sacrificing values, but adopting more 'masculine' traits such as confidence or assertiveness can allow for personal and professional growth. For some people this takes practice! Don't downplay your femininity, but challenge the idea that you have to be any one way because of your gender or experiences.

[3] SPEAK UP.

Some studies show men speak up to 75% of the time in cogendered meetings. If you have an opinion or idea, then say it. Your ideas matter and are as important as your male colleagues'. Your experiences can lead to innovative solutions to problems that some men may not even realize exist. Try to drop qualifiers and apologies from the beginning of sentences. This will allow you to come across as assertive and powerful.

[4] ACCEPT CREDIT FOR YOUR WORK.

You did the work. You made the effort. You succeeded. When the accolades fall on you, don't shy away. You deserve the credit, so accept it (and bask in it).

[5] LIFT YOUR COLLEAGUES UP.

Every woman who walked before you has struggled, but made a path for you. Likewise, your female colleagues struggle in ways you may not be aware. Foster healthy workplaces, strong female teams and relationships. Be a mentor if such a program exists and a leader for women if it doesn't. Remember the things that bothered you throughout your training and education, and try to change it for the generations that follow.

Dr. Alanna Husch is an orthopedic surgeon practising in Corner Brook. Originally from Calgary, she has called Newfoundland home since 2011. Her favourite person is her Labrador retriever, Jude. She enjoys attending concerts, hiking, skiing, snowshoeing, and travelling.

SEPTEMBER

FOCUS ON ONE OF YOUR STRENGTHS

CIRCLE ONE

I'm woke!

Having feelings

I'm awesome!

Idea crush

Fuck the patriarchy!

Did I self-care?

MONDAY	TUESDAY	WEDNESDAY
2	3	4
9	10	11
16	17	18
23 / 30	24	25

WHAT HAVE YOU DONE FOR SELF-CARE THIS MONTH?

HOW DID YOU RESIST?

#FEMINISTFRIDAY
PAY IT FORWARD

THURSDAY	FRIDAY	SATURDAY	SUNDAY
			1
5	6	7	8
12	13	14	15
19	20	21	22
26	27	28	29

NOTES

SEPTEMBER

M	T	W	T	F	S	S
						1
2	3	4	5	6	7	8
9	10	11	12	13	14	15
16	17	18	19	20	21	22
23	24	25	26	27	28	29
30	1	2	3	4	5	6

2 MONDAY

Labour Day

3 TUESDAY

4 WEDNESDAY

THINGS TO DO

WEEKLY GOALS AND NOTES

5 THURSDAY

6 FRIDAY

7 SATURDAY

8 SUNDAY

THOUGHTS AND INSPIRATION

SEPTEMBER

M	T	W	T	F	S	S
						1
2	3	4	5	6	7	8
9	10	11	12	13	14	15
16	17	18	19	20	21	22
23	24	25	26	27	28	29
30	1	2	3	4	5	6

9 MONDAY

10 TUESDAY

11 WEDNESDAY

THINGS TO DO

WEEKLY GOALS AND NOTES

12 THURSDAY

13 FRIDAY

14 SATURDAY

15 SUNDAY

THOUGHTS AND INSPIRATION

SEPTEMBER

SEPTEMBER 17–21 **SEXUAL VIOLENCE AWARENESS WEEK**

M	T	W	T	F	S	S
						1
2	3	4	5	6	7	8
9	10	11	12	13	14	15
16	17	18	19	20	21	22
23	24	25	26	27	28	29
30	1	2	3	4	5	6

16 MONDAY

17 TUESDAY

#ITSNOTOKAY

18 WEDNESDAY

THINGS TO DO

WEEKLY GOALS AND NOTES

19 THURSDAY

20 FRIDAY

21 SATURDAY

22 SUNDAY

THOUGHTS AND INSPIRATION

SEPTEMBER

M	T	W	T	F	S	S
						1
2	3	4	5	6	7	8
9	10	11	12	13	14	15
16	17	18	19	20	21	22
23	24	25	26	27	28	29
30	1	2	3	4	5	6

23 MONDAY

First Day of Fall

24 TUESDAY

25 WEDNESDAY

THINGS TO DO

WEEKLY GOALS AND NOTES

26 THURSDAY

27 FRIDAY

#NLHISTORY In 1894, Margaret Iris Duley was born on this day. She was Newfoundland's first internationally acclaimed novelist.

28 SATURDAY

29 SUNDAY

Navaratri Begins

THOUGHTS AND INSPIRATION

SEPTEMBER

M	T	W	T	F	S	S
						1
2	3	4	5	6	7	8
9	10	11	12	13	14	15
16	17	18	19	20	21	22
23	24	25	26	27	28	29
30	1	2	3	4	5	6

30 MONDAY

Rosh Hashana

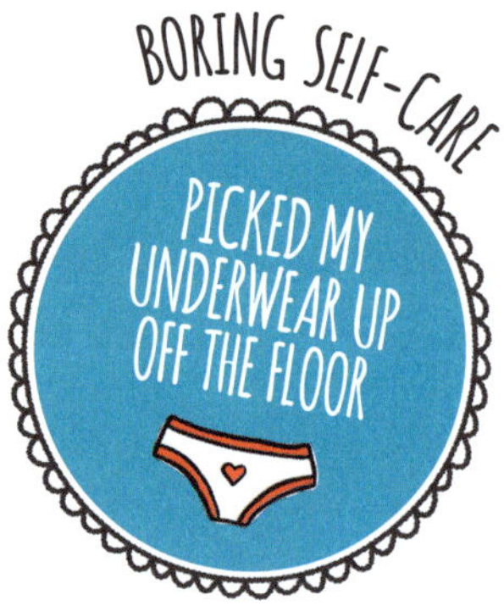

NOTES

SPACE OF INFINITE POSSIBILTY

fem [FIVE]

TOP FIVE REASONS TO RUN FOR MAYOR

Renee Sharpe

[1] YOU GET THE MIC.

Though my running wasn't strategic, I know now that the best way to bring your generally unpopular community activism to the front of the popular discourse is to run for mayor. Conservative men and women will stop you in the shopping aisle of Sobeys to thank you for bringing the decriminalization of sex work and insistence on safe injection sites into the mainstream conversation. They will show a surprising appreciation for your harm reduction, feminist and anti-oppression based mayoral platform.

[2] DESTROY IMPOSTER SYNDROME.

You won't have time to buckle under the relentless weight of feeling like an imposter in a role that is catered to the older white career politician. It is wildly fun to run as a feminist punker, break all the rules, and still do an incredible job despite the odds. Take care of yourself through this process. Learn to ask for help. Your community will do the work and have your back. You will be supported.

[3] YOU LOOK GREAT.

Of course, you must look tight and professional to be taken seriously if we are speaking as working-class women. Comb your hair and get a blazer and feel that hot power of suddenly being heard and valued by the middle/upper class "to do's." NTV's "Question and Answer Period" never looked so good. Don't take out your nose ring though: you're still a shit disturber.

[4] LOVE AND CLOSURE/COMMUNITY BUILDING 101.

Run. Even if you're scared shitless. Your community and family will rally, do the work, and show you the love and support that you never actually thought was there. It's not about you; it's about collectively flipping and rewriting the script and making incredible, powerful, and positive change TOGETHER – and that's hot.

[5] YOU BECOME MAYOR.

Literally. You can become mayor. If you are a woman, Indigenous, gay, trans, marginalized, or under-represented in any way, RUN FOR MAYOR. It's our world. See you in the streets.

Renee Sharpe is a welder with the Iron Workers Union, a Wen-Do Women's Self Defence instructor, a punker and a DIY talk-show host. Renee ran for mayor in the 2017 St. John's municipal election as a working-class feminist, and got almost 14% of the vote. 6000 people voted for a change. We got one. Five incredible women now have a seat at the table, and that feels good. Our work continues towards more diverse representation, and towards safer and stronger communities with no one left out.

OCTOBER

FOCUS ON ONE OF YOUR STRENGTHS

CIRCLE ONE

I'm woke!

Having feelings

I'm awesome!

Idea crush

Fuck the patriarchy!

Did I self-care?

MONDAY	TUESDAY	WEDNESDAY
	1	2
7	8	9
14	15	16
21	22	23
28	29	30

WHAT HAVE YOU DONE FOR SELF-CARE THIS MONTH?

#FEMINISTFRIDAY
PAY IT FORWARD

HOW DID YOU RESIST?

THURSDAY	FRIDAY	SATURDAY	SUNDAY
3	4	5	6
10	11	12	13
17	18	19	20
24	25	26	27
31			

NOTES

OCTOBER

WOMEN'S HISTORY MONTH

M	T	W	T	F	S	S
	1	2	3	4	5	6
7	8	9	10	11	12	13
14	15	16	17	18	19	20
21	22	23	24	25	26	27
28	29	30	31	1	2	3

30 MONDAY

1 TUESDAY

#NLHISTORY In 2013, the Safe Harbour Outreach Project (SHOP) was created.

2 WEDNESDAY

THINGS TO DO

WEEKLY GOALS AND NOTES

3 THURSDAY

4 FRIDAY

Sisters In Spirit (SIS) Vigils: The In Her Name vigil is held at the Colonial Building to remember the missing and murdered women and girls of Newfoundland and Labrador.

5 SATURDAY

6 SUNDAY

THOUGHTS AND INSPIRATION

OCTOBER

WOMEN'S HISTORY MONTH

M	T	W	T	F	S	S
	1	2	3	4	5	6
7	8	9	10	11	12	13
14	15	16	17	18	19	20
21	22	23	24	25	26	27
28	29	30	31	1	2	3

7 MONDAY

Navaratri Ends

8 TUESDAY

Yom Kippur

9 WEDNESDAY

THINGS TO DO

WEEKLY GOALS AND NOTES

10 THURSDAY

11 FRIDAY

International Day of the Girl

#NLHISTORY On this day in 1754, Eleanor Power was the first woman hung in English Canada.

12 SATURDAY

13 SUNDAY

THOUGHTS AND INSPIRATION

OCTOBER

❌ OCTOBER 14–20 **YWCA INTERNATIONAL WEEK WITHOUT VIOLENCE**

M	T	W	T	F	S	S
	1	2	3	4	5	6
7	8	9	10	11	12	13
14	15	16	17	18	19	20
21	22	23	24	25	26	27
28	29	30	31	1	2	3

14 MONDAY

Thanksgiving Day

15 TUESDAY

16 WEDNESDAY

THINGS TO DO

WEEKLY GOALS AND NOTES

17 THURSDAY

18 FRIDAY

Menopause Day
Persons Day

19 SATURDAY

20 SUNDAY

THOUGHTS AND INSPIRATION

OCTOBER

OCTOBER 21–27 **PAP TEST AWARENESS WEEK**

M	T	W	T	F	S	S
	1	2	3	4	5	6
7	8	9	10	11	12	13
14	15	16	17	18	19	20
21	22	23	24	25	26	27
28	29	30	31	1	2	3

21 MONDAY

22 TUESDAY

23 WEDNESDAY

THINGS TO DO

WEEKLY GOALS AND NOTES

24 THURSDAY

25 FRIDAY

26 SATURDAY

27 SUNDAY

Diwali

THOUGHTS AND INSPIRATION

OCTOBER

WOMEN'S HISTORY MONTH

M	T	W	T	F	S	S
	1	2	3	4	5	6
7	8	9	10	11	12	13
14	15	16	17	18	19	20
21	22	23	24	25	26	27
28	29	30	31	1	2	3

28 MONDAY

29 TUESDAY

30 WEDNESDAY

THINGS TO DO

WEEKLY GOALS AND NOTES

31 THURSDAY

Halloween

CHALLENGE YOURSELF TO PRACTICE MORE "BORING SELF-CARE"

Be mindful of the gratification, balance, and purpose these things bring to your life.

TAKE CARE OF YOURSELF. YOU MATTER AND YOU DESERVE IT!

I TOLD HIM I'D REPORT IF HE DIDN'T LET ME GO

Heidi Coombs

In the spring of 1914, Jane H. was boarding in St. John's at the home of George D. and his wife on Notre Dame Street. Jane was a married woman, but her husband was disabled and living with his mother at Battle Harbour. Three of her children were at the International Grenfell Association orphanage in St. Anthony. Jane had been working in St. John's since the fall of 1913.

On Thursday, May 28th, Thomas S. entered the house while Jane was there alone with her baby, and he raped her. George arrived home shortly after the attack. He "saw her downhearted," whereupon she told him what happened and then reported the attack to the police.

The case was heard by the Magistrate in St. John's. Jane's statement was brief – she explained that, "[Thomas] came along and spoke to me. He put his hand under my clothes and on my person. I struggled against him getting up. I told him I'd report if he didn't let me go. He was holding me in and exposed his person."

George also testified and confirmed Jane's statement. He knew Thomas, and thought it strange that he came by the house, since he had only been there once before. About the attack, he stated, "She told me the man knocked her down on the floor and pulled up her clothes and did what he wanted to do with her."

During the trial, the defence called Jane's character into question. Thomas stated that George said he had been with her three times that week. However, George denied this. He confirmed that there were "2 fellows" at the door almost every night during the past week, "And one night she was out till nearly 12 o'clock." But he clarified, "She don't be out every night. I know the girl to be decent."

Thomas was found guilty of the rape and served time at the Penitentiary.

This rape case from 1914 demonstrates similar themes to recent high-profile sexual assault cases in Canada, especially in terms of the propensity of the defence to question the character of the woman involved. In Jane's case, it is not insignificant that she had the unwavering support of another man – a man who was willing to dispute the other man's false statement. Men have been in the past, and are today, important allies for women, for justice, and for challenging the patriarchal structure of our institutions.

Despite significant headway in uncovering women's experiences in Newfoundland and Labrador history, giving voice to those women remains a challenge. As Linda Cullum, Maeve Baird, and Cynthia Penney have pointed out, the patriarchal structure of society and its institutions has historically meant that women were represented "in narrow and limited ways, often with little input from themselves."

Although we only have access to her statement in the form of court minutes, Jane's "voice" from May 1914 rings out. Her courage to report the crime – as a woman alone in St. John's, with a disabled husband and her children living hundreds of miles away – is an inspiration and a testament to the strength of women throughout history.

1 All trial statements from The Rooms Provincial Archives, GN 5-3-A-1, Magistrates Court, Central Circuit, Minutes, Box 211.

2 Linda Cullum and Maeve Baird, with the assistance of Cynthia Penny, "A Woman's Lot: Women and Law in Newfoundland from Early Settlement to the Twentieth Century," in *Pursuing Equality: Historical Perspectives on Women in Newfoundland and Labrador*, Linda Kealey, ed., (St. John's: Institute of Social and Economic Research, 1993), p. 67.

Photo by Ritche Perez

Heidi Coombs is an historian, actor, and filmmaker from St. John's. She has a PhD in history and is currently vice-president of the Newfoundland and Labrador Historical Society. Her first short film, *Life's Short. Wear the Sparkly Earrings*, premiered at the St. John's International Women's Film Festival in 2017.

NOVEMBER

FOCUS ON ONE OF YOUR STRENGTHS

CIRCLE ONE

I'm woke!

Having feelings

I'm awesome!

Idea crush

Fuck the patriarchy!

Did I self-care?

MONDAY	TUESDAY	WEDNESDAY
4	5	6
11	12	13
18	19	20
25	26	27

WHAT HAVE YOU DONE FOR SELF-CARE THIS MONTH?

#FEMINISTFRIDAY
PAY IT FORWARD

HOW DID YOU RESIST?

THURSDAY	FRIDAY	SATURDAY	SUNDAY
	1	2	3
7	8	9	10
14	15	16	17
21	22	23	24
28	29	30	

NOTES

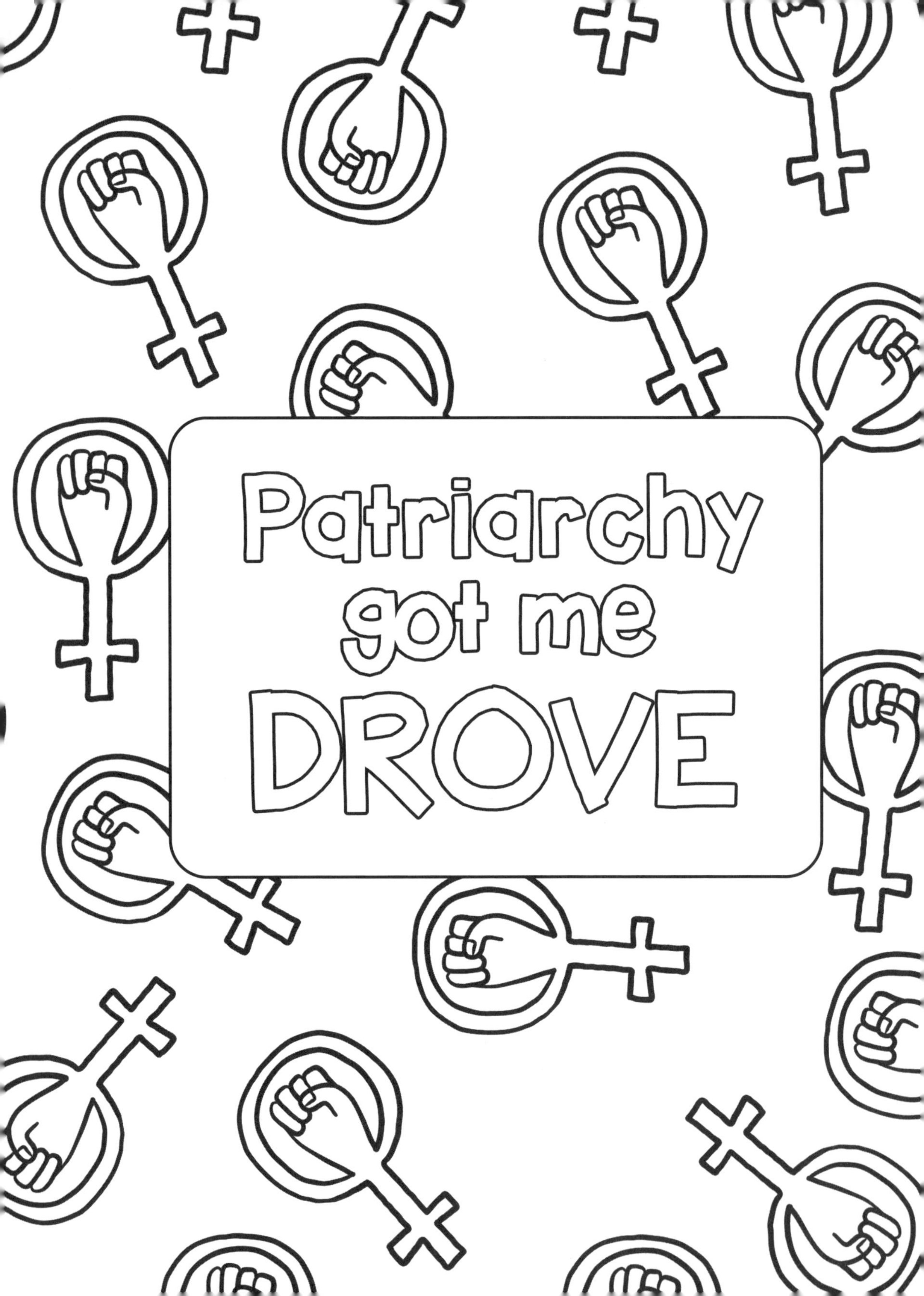
Patriarchy
got me
DROVE

NOVEMBER

M	T	W	T	F	S	S
				1	2	3
4	5	6	7	8	9	10
11	12	13	14	15	16	17
18	19	20	21	22	23	24
25	26	27	28	29	30	1

31 THURSDAY

Halloween

1 FRIDAY

2 SATURDAY

#NLHISTORY On this date in 2015, the St. John's Status of Women Council organized the first women's debate, featuring the leaders of the three main political parties, in the lead up to the provincial election.

3 SUNDAY

Daylight Savings Time Ends

THOUGHTS AND INSPIRATION

NOVEMBER

M	T	W	T	F	S	S
				1	2	3
4	5	6	7	8	9	10
11	12	13	14	15	16	17
18	19	20	21	22	23	24
25	26	27	28	29	30	1

4 MONDAY

5 TUESDAY

Guy Fawkes Night (Bonfire Night)

6 WEDNESDAY

THINGS TO DO

WEEKLY GOALS AND NOTES

7 THURSDAY

8 FRIDAY

9 SATURDAY

10 SUNDAY

THOUGHTS AND INSPIRATION

NOVEMBER

M	T	W	T	F	S	S
				1	2	3
4	5	6	7	8	9	10
11	12	13	14	15	16	17
18	19	20	21	22	23	24
25	26	27	28	29	30	1

11 MONDAY

Remembrance Day

12 TUESDAY

13 WEDNESDAY

THINGS TO DO

WEEKLY GOALS AND NOTES

14 THURSDAY

15 FRIDAY

16 SATURDAY

17 SUNDAY

THOUGHTS AND INSPIRATION

NOVEMBER

M	T	W	T	F	S	S
				1	2	3
4	5	6	7	8	9	10
11	12	13	14	15	16	17
18	19	20	21	22	23	24
25	26	27	28	29	30	1

18 MONDAY

19 TUESDAY

20 WEDNESDAY

National Child's Day
Transgender Day of Remembrance

THINGS TO DO

WEEKLY GOALS AND NOTES

21 THURSDAY

22 FRIDAY

23 SATURDAY

24 SUNDAY

THOUGHTS AND INSPIRATION

NOVEMBER

M	T	W	T	F	S	S
				1	2	3
4	5	6	7	8	9	10
11	12	13	14	15	16	17
18	19	20	21	22	23	24
25	26	27	28	29	30	1

25 MONDAY

International Day of the Elimination of Violence Against Women

26 TUESDAY

27 WEDNESDAY

THINGS TO DO

WEEKLY GOALS AND NOTES

28 THURSDAY

29 FRIDAY

30 SATURDAY

DECEMBER

1 SUNDAY

World AIDS Day

THOUGHTS AND INSPIRATION

fem [FIVE]

TOP FIVE

WOMEN MUSICIANS UNDER 25

Wendy Rose

When asked by the St. John's Status of Women Council about writing for the 2019 Woman's Almanac, I was thrilled. My assignment: a "top five list of something related to women and music in the province." Top five? How could I possibly pick five that would accurately reflect the abundance of talented women in the province's music industry? For every name that popped into my head, another 10 followed. Two days of brainstorming culminated in this submission, highlighting five women musicians under 25. These fierce females are intelligent, driven, and talented. Remember their names, hear their music, and learn their stories.

[1] THE ANTLE SISTERS

Mary and Ella have a special bond: the 15-year-old twins have been creating music since preschool, playing instruments like ukulele, guitar, accordion, flute, and saxophone. After years of involvement in musical theatre, the pair began performing as a folk duo in 2016. The sisters have performed at the Folk Arts Society Holiday Wassail, the TD Music Corner, the JBR Up & Comers Evening, and more.

[2] BRIDGET AND DAHLIA

Bridget Swift and Dahlia Waller showcased their impressive musicality at the 2017 Newfoundland and Labrador Folk Festival, a performance earned by their win at MusicNL's Newfound Talent Competition. The two 16-year-old west coasters released an EP titled *Wooden Castles*, and have played at the Rotary Arts Centre, The Gathering, the Feast of Cohen, and opened for Fortunate Ones in Corner Brook.

[3] RACHEL COUSINS

Sing NL 2017 winner Rachel Cousins is one busy 17-year-old. The singer/songwriter was a semi-finalist in the Unsigned Only international songwriting competition, has been nominated for MusicNL's Female Artist of the Year and Rising Star awards, and has performed on more than 100 stages with Canadian stars. Her debut album, *This Fire*, was released August 2017.

[4] CLARE FOLLETT

A multi-instrumentalist singer, songwriter, and producer, Clare Follett, 16, is from St. John's. Clare's impressive talent has brought her to stages across the province and as far as Trinidad, as the winner of Club One New Releases' high-school musician contest. Her successful debut album, *Neck Deep*, was released in 2017 and earned Clare the title of MusicNL's Pop/Rock Artist of the Year, Songwriter of the Year, and the Rising Star of the Year award.

[5] ROSEMARY LAWTON

A MUN School of Music graduate, 23-year-old Rosemary Lawton knows her trade. Rosemary has shared her fiddle and violin skills with the Newfoundland Symphony Orchestra, the MUN Chamber Orchestra, the Celtic Fiddlers, the Derina Harvey Band, and more. Fusing her love of classical and traditional music, Rosemary released her debut EP *Painted Glass* in December 2017. She has since joined Rod Jackson and The Perfect Strangers, continuing to hone her impressive musical and vocal capabilities.

Wendy Rose is a freelance journalist based in St. John's, NL. Focusing primarily on arts and lifestyles, she has written for local media outlets such as *The Telegram*, *The Newfoundland Herald*, *Downhome Magazine*, *The Overcast*, *Secret East*, CBC, and CBC Arts. You can find Wendy wherever the local arts and culture is. Since August 2016, she has been *The Telegram*'s main live-event reviewer for music, theatre, contemporary dance, film, ballet, festivals, performance art, and more. This interest and involvement in the local arts scene pairs beautifully with her job at Fred's Records, where she has worked for three years. On the rare occasion that she's not writing for one of many local media outlets, taking in a show, or working at Fred's or Tvål Skincare, Wendy can be found on her couch, binge-watching PVR'd episodes of Jeopardy.

DECEMBER

FOCUS ON ONE OF YOUR STRENGTHS

CIRCLE ONE

I'm woke!

Having feelings

I'm awesome!

Idea crush

Fuck the patriarchy!

Did I self-care?

MONDAY	TUESDAY	WEDNESDAY
2	3	4
9	10	11
16	17	18
23 / 30	24 / 31	25

WHAT HAVE YOU DONE FOR SELF-CARE THIS MONTH?

#FEMINISTFRIDAY
PAY IT FORWARD

HOW DID YOU RESIST?

THURSDAY	FRIDAY	SATURDAY	SUNDAY
			1
5	6	7	8
12	13	14	15
19	20	21	22
26	27	28	29

NOTES

DECEMBER

M	T	W	T	F	S	S
						1
2	3	4	5	6	7	8
9	10	11	12	13	14	15
16	17	18	19	20	21	22
23	24	25	26	27	28	29
30	31	1	2	3	4	5

2 MONDAY

3 TUESDAY

International Day of Persons with Disabilities

#NLHISTORY On this date in 2010, Kathy Dunderdale became the first female premier of Newfoundland and Labrador.

4 WEDNESDAY

THINGS TO DO

WEEKLY GOALS AND NOTES

5 THURSDAY

6 FRIDAY

National Day of Remembrance and Action on Violence Against Women

7 SATURDAY

8 SUNDAY

THOUGHTS AND INSPIRATION

DECEMBER

M	T	W	T	F	S	S
						1
2	3	4	5	6	7	8
9	10	11	12	13	14	15
16	17	18	19	20	21	22
23	24	25	26	27	28	29
30	31	1	2	3	4	5

9 MONDAY

10 TUESDAY

11 WEDNESDAY

THINGS TO DO

WEEKLY GOALS AND NOTES

12 THURSDAY

13 FRIDAY

14 SATURDAY

15 SUNDAY

THOUGHTS AND INSPIRATION

DECEMBER

M	T	W	T	F	S	S
						1
2	3	4	5	6	7	8
9	10	11	12	13	14	15
16	17	18	19	20	21	22
23	24	25	26	27	28	29
30	31	1	2	3	4	5

16 MONDAY

17 TUESDAY

International Day to End Violence Against Sex Workers

18 WEDNESDAY

THINGS TO DO

WEEKLY GOALS AND NOTES

19 THURSDAY

20 FRIDAY

21 SATURDAY

First Day of Winter

22 SUNDAY

First Day of Hanukkah

THOUGHTS AND INSPIRATION

DECEMBER

M	T	W	T	F	S	S
						1
2	3	4	5	6	7	8
9	10	11	12	13	14	15
16	17	18	19	20	21	22
23	24	25	26	27	28	29
30	31	1	2	3	4	5

23 MONDAY

Tibb's Eve (Tipp's Eve)

24 TUESDAY

Christmas Eve

25 WEDNESDAY

Christmas Day

THINGS TO DO

WEEKLY GOALS AND NOTES

26 THURSDAY

Boxing Day | St. Stephen's Day (The traditional beginning of mummering in Newfoundland communities)

27 FRIDAY

28 SATURDAY

29 SUNDAY

THOUGHTS AND INSPIRATION

DECEMBER

M	T	W	T	F	S	S
						1
2	3	4	5	6	7	8
9	10	11	12	13	14	15
16	17	18	19	20	21	22
23	24	25	26	27	28	29
30	31	1	2	3	4	5

30 MONDAY

Last Day of Hanukkah

31 TUESDAY

New Year's Eve

NOTES

HOUSE FIRE

Emily Carrigan

My body is not a house
you will find no staircases winding themselves up my backbone
no chimney sticking up behind my ears
there are no windows behind my eyes that you can peer out of
no floorboards nailed into the soles of my feet
My body is not the building you go home to at night
I do not protect against the rain or the wind or the snow
I do not have fluffy pink insulation between my walls
I do not have walls!
There is no kitchen in my belly
no stove hidden inside my beating heart
I am not made of wood
Fire is not my sworn enemy
you will not watch me crumble under heavy flames because you left
the candles burning in the living room
I will not go up in smoke
No one will scream Fire!
Which is why
no one will come running to save me
No one
will come running
to save
me

So, scream of imaginary flames
as his hands burn the skin of your wrists
as you choke on his smoky black breath
This body does not warrant rescue
this body probably deserved it
probably flirted too much, wore too short of a dress
knew him from before
said yes to him before
there is no fire-escape for your mind to go down
no bouncing net to catch you
a house does not collapse in on itself to escape, it's just collapsing
a house does not cry out for the ashes it has become
a house would never crumble so quickly

Emily Carrigan is a spoken-word poet from St. John's, NL. She is a past organizer of Spoken Word St. John's poetry open mic nights and performed her own work at those events since they began 5 years ago. Emily has also been asked to perform at such events as FemFest, The Vagina Monologues, Slut Walk, and the Women's Work Festival.

SPACE OF INFINITE POSSIBILTY

WOMEN SERVING ORGANIZATIONS

REGIONAL COORDINATING COMMITTEES AGAINST VIOLENCE

Burin Peninsula Voice Against Violence | Krista Foote, Executive Director
60 Atlantic Crescent, P.O. Box 87 | Marystown, NL | A0E 2M0
T (709) 279-4030 **F** (709) 279-5387 **E** bpvav@nf.aibn.com

Violence Prevention, Avalon East | Valerie Barter, Executive Director
31 Peet Street, Tara Place, Suite 215 | St. John's, NL | A1B 3W8
T (709) 757-0137 **F** (709) 754-4949 **E** cavae.save.now@gmail.com

Communities Against Violence | Stacy Harris, Executive Director
30A Cathedral Street, P.O. Box 250 | Harbour Grace, NL | A0A 2M0
T (709) 596-0726 **F** (709) 596-3321 **E** info@communitiesagainstviolence.org

Eastern Region Committee Against Violence | Tracey Fleming, Executive Director
105 Manitoba Drive, Suite 304 | Clarenville, NL | A5A 1K2
T (709) 466-4676 **F** (709) 466-4670 **E** ercav@gov.nl.ca

Northern Committee Against Violence | Darlene Rice, Executive Director
279 West Street, P.O. Box 847 | St. Anthony, NL | A0K 4S0
T (709) 454-3351 **F** (709) 454-2334 **E** darlenerice@gov.nl.ca

Roads to End Violence | Lori Oram, Executive Director
157 Airport Boulevard | Gander, NL | A1V 1K6
T (709) 651-2250 **F** (709) 651-2295 **E** info@roadstoendviolence.ca

Southwestern Coalition to End Violence | Bernice Hancock, Coordinating Agency Representative
31-37 Gallant Street, P.O. Box 621 | Stephenville, NL | A2N 3B5
T (709) 643-1022 **F** (709) 643-2293 **E** swceviolence@gmail.com

Violence Prevention West | Victoria Jones, Executive Director
98 Broadway | Corner Brook, NL | A2H 4W1
T (709) 634-6606 **F** (709) 639-1093 **E** violencepreventionwest@gmail.com

Violence Prevention Labrador | Petrina Beals, Executive Director
P.O. Box 869, Stn B | Happy Valley-Goose Bay, NL | A0P 1E0
T (709) 899-3231 **F** (709) 931-2601 **E** coordinator@vplabrador.ca

Violence Prevention South and Central | Katherine Arnold, Executive Director
5 Hardy Avenue | Grand Falls-Windsor, NL | A2A 2P8
T (709) 489-8828 **F** (709) 489-8620 **E** ed@vpsc.ca

WOMEN'S CENTRES/COUNCILS

Bay St. George Status of Women Council | Janice Kennedy, Executive Director
P.O. Box 501 | Stephenville, NL | A2N 3B4
T (709) 643-4444 **F** (709) 643-4707 **E** executivedirector.bsgswc@gmail.com

Corner Brook Status of Women Council | Paula Sheppard Thibeau
P.O. Box 373 | Corner Brook, NL | A2H 6E3
T (709) 639-8522 F (709) 639-1093 E cbwomenscentre@gmail.com

Gander Status of Women Council | Sandra McKellar
61 Elizabeth Drive, 1st Floor, Polaris Bldg. | Gander, NL | A1V 1G4
T (709) 256-4395 F (709) 256-7767 E women.gander@nf.aibn.com

Gateway Status of Women Council | Tanya Hawco
P.O. Box 1359 | Port aux Basques, NL | A0M 1C0
T (709) 695-7505 F (709) 695-9756 E gswc@nf.aibn.com

Labrador West Status of Women Council | Michelene Gray, Executive Director
P.O. Box 171 | Labrador City, NL | A2V 2K5
T (709) 944-6562 F (709) 944-4078 E lwsw@crrstv.net

Mokami Status of Women Council | Raelene Vickers, Executive Director
P.O. Box 329, Stn. B | Happy Valley-Goose Bay, NL | A0P 1E0
T (709) 896-3484, ext. 202 F (709) 896-3472 E programs@mokamiwomen.ca

St. John's Status of Women Council | Jenny Wright, Executive Director
170 Cashin Avenue Extension | St. John's, NL | A1E 3B6
T (709) 753-0220 F (709) 753-3817 E jenny@sjwomenscentre.ca

Status of Women Central | Jackie Thompson
5B Bayley Street | Grand Falls-Windsor, NL | A2A 2T5
T (709) 489-8919 F (709) 489-8981 E coordinator.sowc@bellaliant.com

TRANSITION HOUSES

Cara Transition House | Ann Marie Connors, Executive Director
P.O. Box 305 | Gander, NL | A1V 1W7
T (709) 256-9306 F (709) 256-6130 E administration@carahouse.com

Willow House | Heather Davis, Executive Director
P.O. Box 152 | Corner Brook, NL | A2H 6C9
T (709) 634-4199 F (709) 634-4197 E info@transitionhouse.ca

Grace Sparkes House | Lisa Slaney, Executive Director
P.O. Box 327 | Marystown, NL | A0E 2M0
T (709) 279-3560 F (709) 279-3780 E lslaney@gracesparkeshouse.com

Hope Haven | Nicole Northcott, Executive Director
350 Booth Avenue | Labrador City, NL | A2V 2K1
T (709) 944-7124 F (709) 944-7747 E hopehaven@crrstv.net

Iris Kirby House | Michelle Greene, Executive Director
196 Waterford Bridge Road | St. John's, NL | A1E 1E2
T (709) 722-8272 F (709) 722-0164 E michellegreene@iriskirbyhouse.ca

Kirkina House | Marie Rich, Executive Director
P.O. Box 59 | Rigolet, Nunatsiavut, NL | A0P 1P0
T (709) 947-3334 F (709) 947-3583 E rigoletsafehouse@bellaliant.com

Libra House I Jessica Keating, Executive Director
P.O. Box 449, Stn. B I Happy Valley-Goose Bay, NL I A0P 1E0
T (709) 896-8022 F (709) 896-8223 E jkeating@librahouse.ca

O'Shaughnessy House I Kelly Fewer, Manager of Programs
P.O. Box 497 I Carbonear, NL I A1Y 1B9
T (709) 596-8208 F (709) 596-8003 E kellyfewer@iriskirbyhouse.nf.net

Nain Transition House I Nicole Dicker, Executive Director
P.O. Box 447 I Nain, NL I A0P 1L0
T (709) 922-1230 F (709) 922-1424 E nainsafehouse@nf.aibn.com

Naomi Centre (Stella's Circle) I Lisa Browne, CEO
4 Patrick Street I St. John's, NL I A1E 2S6
T (709) 738-5909 F (709) 738-7808 E l.browne@stellascircle.ca

Natuashish Safe House I Rose Poker, Coordinator
Natuashish, NL T (709) 478-2390 F (709) 478-2392 E kbenuen@gmail.com

Nukum Munik Shelter I Frances Nui, Executive Director
Sheshatshiu, NL T (709) 497-8868 F (709) 497-8827 E mpia@sifn.ca

Wiseman Centre I 714 Water Street I St. John's, NL I A1E 1C1
T (709) 739-8355 F (709) 739-0330 E lloyd_george@can.salvationarmy.org

OTHER STAKEHOLDERS

AIDS Committee of Newfoundland and Labrador I Gerard Yetman, Executive Director
47 Janeway Place I St. John's, NL I A1A 1R7
T (709) 579-8656 F (709) 579-0559 E gyetman@acnl.net
Western Office I Jessica Hackett, Harm Reduction Manager T (709) 634-7927

Association for New Canadians I Megan Morris, Executive Director
144 Military Road, P.O. Box 2031, Stn. C I St. John's, NL I A1C 5R6
T (709) 722-9680 F (709) 754-4407 E diversity@nfld.net
Karen Glavine, Settlement Social Worker I socialworker@nfld.net
Corner Brook Office I Kevin Walsh T (709) 634-2653 E kwalsh@ancnl.ca

Athena Health Centre I Rolanda Ryan, Owner
Unit 50 Hamlyn Road Plaza, Suite 408 I St. John's, NL I A1E 5X7
T (709) 754-3572 F (709) 754-6626 E athenahealthcentre@bellaliant.com

Boys and Girls Club of Newfoundland and Labrador I Jason Fleming, Club Manager
P.O. Box 5012 I St. John's, NL I A1C 5V3
T (709) 579-0181, ext. 102 E jfleming@bgcstjohns.ca

Canadian Mental Health Association of Newfoundland and Labrador
Dan Goodyear, Chief Executive Officer
603 Topsail Road I St. John's, NL I A1E 2E1
T (709) 753-8550 F (709) 753-8537 E dgoodyear@cmhanl.ca
Tianna Butler, Western Regional Coordinator
157 Minnesota Drive, P.O. Box 17 I Stephenville, NL I A2N 2Y7
T (709) 643-5553 F (709) 643-5122

Tia Morris, Coordinator
16 Pinsent Drive, P.O. Box 542 | Grand Falls-Windsor, NL | A2A 2J9
T (709) 489-3302 **F** (709) 489-3710 **E** tmorris@cmhanl.ca

Coalition of Persons with Disabilities | Emily Christy, Executive Director
460 Torbay Road | St. John's, NL | A1A 5J3
T (709) 722-7011 **E** info@codnl.ca

Consumers' Health Awareness Network Newfoundland and Labrador (CHANNAL)
Mike Herrell, Coordinator
284 LeMarchant Road | St. John's, NL | A1E 1R2
T (709) 753-2560 **F** (709) 753-1109 **E** mherrell@channal.ca
CHANNAL (Regional)
Bonnie Rotchford, Regional Peer Support | Western
108 Carolina Avenue, Suite 1 | Stephenville, NL | A2N 2S4
T (709) 643-4361 **E** brotchford@channal.ca

Empower NL | Joby Fleming, Advocacy Coordinator
4 Escasoni Place | St. John's, NL | A1A 3R6
T (709) 722-4031 **F** (709) 722-0147 **E** joby@empowernl.ca

Human Rights Commission | Carey Majid, Executive Director
21 Crosbie Place, The Beothuk Building | St. John's, NL | A1B 4J6
T (709) 729-2709 **F** (709) 729-0790 **E** careymajid@gov.nl.ca

Multicultural Women's Organization of Newfoundland and Labrador
Kaberi Sarma-Debnath, Executive Director
44 Torbay Road, Nuport Building, Box #9 | St. John's, NL | A1A 2G4
T (709) 726-0321 **F** (709) 726-0322 **E** kaberi.debnath@gmail.com

Newfoundland and Labrador Sexual Assault Crisis and Prevention Centre
Nicole Kieley, Executive Director
31 Peet Street, Suite 223 | St. John's, NL | A1B 3W8
T (709) 747-7757 **F** (709) 747-7758 **E** executivedirector@endsexualviolence.com

Planned Parenthood/Newfoundland and Labrador Sexual Health Centre
Nikki Baldwin, Executive Director
203 Merrymeeting Road | St. Johns, NL | A1C 2W6
T (709) 579-1009 | (877) 666-9847 **F** (709) 726-2308 **E** executivedirector@ppnlshc.com

Provincial Advisory Council on the Status of Women
15 Hallett Crescent, Suite 103 | St. John's, NL | A1B 4C4
T (709) 753-6124

Public Legal Information Association of Newfoundland | Kevin O'Shea, Executive Director
31 Peet Street, Tara Place, Suite 227 | St. John's, NL | A1B 3W8
T (709) 722-2643 **F** (709) 722-0054 **E** director@publiclegalinfo.com

Refugee and Immigrant Advisory Council | Adriana Costano, Coordinator
204 Water Street, Suite 3000 | St. John's, NL | A1C 1A9
T (709) 754-4122 **F** (709) 754-4102 **E** cntct@riac.ca

Seniors Resource Centre of Newfoundland and Labrador | Ms. Kelly Heisz, Executive Director
370 Torbay Road, Suite W 100 | St. John's, NL | A1A 3W8
T (709) 737-2333 F (709) 737-3717 E info@seniorsresource.ca
Elizabeth Siegel, NLNPEA Coordinator
T (709) 737-2333 F (709) 737-3717 E elizabeths@seniorsresource.ca

Transition House Association of Newfoundland and Labrador | Dan Meades, Executive Director
510 Topsail Road, Suite 113 | St. John's, NL | A1E 2C2
T (709) 739-6759 | (709) 330-6810 F (709) 739-6951 E danmeades@thanl.org

YWCA St. John's | Wendolyn Schlamp, Executive Director
31 Peet Street, Suite 217 | St. John's, NL | A1B 3W8
T (709) 726-9922 E info@ywcaststjohns.ca

ABORIGINAL GOVERNMENTS AND ORGANIZATIONS

AnanauKatiget Tumingit Regional Inuit Women's Association
Kim Campbell McLean, Executive Director
P.O. Box 91 | North West River, NL | A0P 1M0
T (709) 497-8100 F (709) 497-8288 E executivedirector@labradorinuitwomen.com

Innu Nation | Gregory Rich, Grand Chief
P.O. Box 119 | Sheshatshiu, NL | A0P 1M0
T (709) 896-1660 E gregory.rich@innu.ca
Dominic Rich T (709) 899-2463
Etienne Rich, Sheshatshiu Deputy Grand Chief T (709) 897-5730 E erich@innu.ca

Labrador Aboriginal Affairs | Franca Smith
21 Broomfield Street | Happy Valley-Goose Bay, NL | A0P 1E0
T (709) 896-1780 F (709) 896-0045 E francasmith@gov.nl.ca
Michelle Watkins, Director E michellewatkins@gov.nl.ca

Labrador Friendship Centre
Jennifer Hefler-Elson, Executive Director | Alica Neville, Program Staff
49 Grenfell Street, P.O. Box 767, Stn. B | Happy Valley-Goose Bay, NL | A0P 1E0
T (709) 896-8302, ext. 222 F (709) 896-8731 E jelson@lfchvgb.ca

Miawpukek First Nation | Mi'sel Joe, Chief
50 Miawpukek Drive, P.O. Box 10 | Conne River, NL | A0H 1J0
T (709) 882-2470 F (709) 882-2292 E saqamaw@mfngov.ca
Cynthia Benoit E cynthiabenoit@crhss.com

Mushuau Innu First Nation | Gregory Rich, Chief
P.O. Box 190 | Natuashish, NL | A0P 1A0
T (709) 478-8827 F (709) 478-8833 E kanikue@gmail.com
Justine Noah, Business Development Officer T (709) 478-8943 E jnoah@innu.ca

Newfoundland Aboriginal Women's Network | Sharon Williston, Executive Director
90 Main Street | Stephenville, NL | A2N 3P8
T (709) 643-4563 F (709) 643-1290
E nawn@nf.aibn.com | executivedirector.nawn2016@gmail.com

Nunatsiavut Government I Johannes Lampe, President
25 Ikajuktauvik Road, P.O. Box 70 I Nain, NL I A0P 1L0
E president@nunatsiavut.com
Roberta Baikie Anderson, Program Director
28 Harmony Road I Makkovik, NL
T (709) 923-2105, ext. 206 E roberta.baikie-andersen@nunatsiavut.com
Brenda Jararuse, Director
1A Hillcrest Road I Happy Valley-Goose Bay, NL I A0P 1C0
T (709) 896-8582, ext. 268 E brenda.jararuse@nunatsiavut.com

NunatuKavut Community Council I Todd Russell, President
P.O. Box 460 Stn. C I Happy Valley-Goose Bay, NL I A0P 1C0
T (709) 896-0592 F (709) 896-0594 E trussell@nunatukavut.ca
Dorothy Earle, CEO T (709) 896-0592, ext. 228 F (709) 896-0594 E dearle@nunatukavut.ca
Frank Holly, Executive Assistant E executiveasst@nunatukavut.ca

Qalipu Mi'Kmaq First Nation Band I Brendan Mitchell, Chief
3 Church Street I Corner Brook, NL I A2H 2Z4
T (709) 634-0996 F (709) 693-3997 E bmitchell@qalipu.ca
Erica Samms-Hurley, Nurse Educator E ehurley@grenfell.mun.ca
Sherry Dean I 95 Brookfield Drive I Corner Brook, NL
T (709) 634-0009 E sherry.dean55@gmail.com

Sheshatshiu Innu First Nation I Eugene Hart, Chief
P.O. Box 160 I Sheshatshiu, NL I A0P 1M0
T (709) 497-8247 F (709) 497-8166 E ehart@sifn.ca
Mary Pia Benuen, Coordinator E mpia@sifn.ca

St. John's Native Friendship Centre I Christopher Sheppard, Executive Director
716 Water Street I St. John's, NL I A1E 1C1
T (709) 726-5902 F (709) 722-0874
E executivedirector@sjnfc.com I csheppard@sjnfc.com

The Temiskaming Native Women's Support Group I Arlene Hache, Program Developer
T (867) 445-1121 E arleneh10@hotmail.com

PROVINCIAL GOVERNMENT DEPARTMENTS AND AGENCIES

Department of Advanced Education, Skills and Labour I Hon. Al Hawkins, Minister
P.O. Box 8700 I St. John's, NL I A1B 4J6
T (709) 729-3580 F (709) 729-6996 E allanhawkins@gov.nl.ca

Department of Tourism, Culture, Industry and Innovation
Hon. Christopher Mitchelmore, Minister
P.O. Box 8700 I St. John's, NL I A1B 4J6
T (709) 729-4728 F (709) 729-0654 E janicehalliday@gov.nl.ca

Department of Children, Seniors and Social Development I Hon. Lisa Dempster, Minister
P.O. Box 8700 I St. John's, NL I A1B 4J6
T (709) 729-0659 F (709) 729-1049 E cssdminister@gov.nl.ca

Department of Education and Early Childhood Development I Hon. Al Hawkins, Minister
P.O. Box 8700 I St. John's, NL I A1B 4J6
T (709) 729-5040 F (709) 729-6996 E janetcormey@gov.nl.ca

Department of Fisheries and Land Resources I Hon. Gerry Byrne, Minister
P.O. Box 8700 I St. John's, NL I A1B 4J6
T (709) 729-3705 F (709) 729-0360 E flrminister@gov.nl.ca

Department of Health and Community Services I Hon. Dr. John Haggie, Minister
P.O. Box 8700 I St. John's, NL I A1B 4J6
T (709) 729-3124 E colleenp@gov.nl.ca

Department of Justice and Public Safety I Hon. Andrew Parsons, Minister
P.O. Box 8700 I St. John's, NL I A1B 4J6
T (709) 729-2869 F (709) 729-0469 E rhondas@gov.nl.ca

Department of Municipal Affairs and Environment I Hon. Andrew Parsons, Minister (Acting)
P.O. Box 8700 I St. John's, NL I A1B 4J6
T (709) 729-3048 F (709) 729-0943 E maeinfo@gov.nl.ca

Department of Natural Resources I Hon. Siobhan Coady, Minister
P.O. Box 8700 I St. John's, NL I A1B 4J6
T (709) 729-2920 F (709) 729-0059 E nrminister@gov.nl.ca

Department of Transportation and Works I Hon. Steve Crocker, Minister
P.O. Box 8700 I St. John's, NL I A1B 4J6
T (709) 729-3679 F (709) 729-4285 E twminister@gov.nl.ca

Labrador Affairs Office I Hon. Dwight Ball, Minister
P.O. Box 3014, Stn. B I Happy Valley-Goose Bay, NL I A0P 1E0
T (709) 896-1780 F (709) 896-0045 E janicebarnes@gov.nl.ca
Intergovernmental and Indigenous Affairs
T (709) 729-2134 I T (709) 729-4776 F (709) 729-5038 I F (709) 729-4900

Newfoundland and Labrador Housing Corporation I Jenny Bowring, Manager
P.O. Box 220 I St. John's, NL I A1C 5J2
T (709) 724-3055 F (709) 724-3250 E jmbowring@nlhc.nl.ca

Office of Climate Change I Hon. Andrew Parsons, Minister
P.O. Box 8700 I St. John's, NL I A1B 4J6
T (709) 729-1210 E climatechange@gov.nl.ca

Office of Public Engagement I Premier Dwight Ball
P.O. Box 8700 I St. John's, NL I A1B 4J6
T (709) 729-1125 F (709) 729-2226

Royal Canadian Mounted Police I Mr. Andrew Boland, Chief Superintendent
100E White Hills Road I Pleasantville, NL I A1A 3T5 T (709) 772-5400

Royal Newfoundland Constabulary I Mr. Joe Boland, Chief
1 Fort Townshend I St. John's, NL I A1C 2G2 T (709) 729-8151

Service NL I Hon. Sherry Gambin-Walsh, Minister
P.O. Box 8700 I St. John's, NL I A1B 4J6
T (709) 729-4712 F (709) 729-4754 E sherrygambinwalsh@gov.nl.ca